Bitcoin: Unlicensed Gambling

Bob Seeman
Roger Svensson

CyberCurb

ISBN: 9798532267220

Cover design by: CyberCurb

Publisher: CyberCurb, Vancouver

Second edition

"All that glitters is not gold."

— derived from William Shakespeare

About the authors

Bob Seeman

Bob Seeman is an entrepreneur and technology, legal and business advisor. He is a Principal at Endeavor which identifies and industrializes game changing technology for the US Government. He is also a co-founder of RIWI Corp., a data analytics company listed on the Toronto Venture Exchange (TSXV: RIWI), has advised government on technology and business issues, and has been a consultant to a bitcoin technology company.

He is a California attorney, electrical engineer and entrepreneur, was a Head of Strategy for Microsoft in London and a technical consultant to the European Commission.

Bob previously practiced administrative law with an international law firm. He holds a Bachelor of Applied Science (Elec. Eng.) with Honours from the University of Toronto, a Master of Business Administration from EDHEC, and a Juris Doctor (J.D.) from the University of British Columbia.

Roger Svensson

Roger Svensson is a senior research fellow and associate professor of economics, working at The Research Institute of Industrial Economics (IFN), an independent research institute in Stockholm, Sweden.

His research focuses on historical monetary systems, monetary policy, innovation economics and government interventions to influence innovation and research and development. He has published many books about these topics as well as several articles in world-leading peer-review scientific journals, such as Research Policy, International Economic Review, The Economic History Review and Journal of Business Venturing.

He has frequently been engaged by both government authorities and private organizations as an investigator into public research and development and innovation support systems as well as intellectual property rights.

Chapters

Appendices

Chapter 1

Introduction

At the dawn of the internet in the late 1990s, people argued that there was now a "new economy" and that there were new profit rules for online companies known then as ".com" companies. One new rule was that the value of online retail companies was based largely on their number of users and less on their profits or near-term prospects of profits. Accordingly, many such unprofitable companies went public on major exchanges. Most of those companies failed and many average individual investors lost a lot of money.

In 1998 - 2000, some people were saying that all the ".com" businesses were merely a bubble. However, the internet has transformed business and transformed our world, largely for the better. We could not have come through the COVID-19 pandemic so well in the West without .com businesses. Some companies, like Amazon, have succeeded massively since the .com bubble burst in 2000 and continue to do so. However, the joke in 1998 was that "Amazon lost money on every transaction... but made it up in volume."

Similar to the claims that .coms were a "new economy", promoters of bitcoin and other cryptocurrencies claim that bitcoin is the "new money". They argue that new rules should apply for money and payments and, since bitcoin abandons intermediaries, transaction costs for payments could be reduced. Another claim is that bitcoin is "digital gold" and will replace gold as a safe asset. Will bitcoin become a successful Amazon.com or a failed Pets.com?

1.1.   Aim and scope of this book

The general aim of this book is to dissect the bitcoin promoters' claims and explain what bitcoin really is. There are many cryptocurrencies but we will focus on the most important and popular, bitcoin. By using economic theory about money and financial assets, we analyse the functions and conditions of money and assets. The first aim of this book is to analyse to what degree bitcoin meets the conditions and functions of money and assets. Based on this analysis, we conclude that the only function of bitcoin that remains is as unlicensed gambling where new players redeem those who entered earlier. It is a zero-sum game.

There is no question that the bitcoin network has been extremely successful. Therefore, a second aim of this book is to analyse the successful methods that bitcoin promoters use. These methods include distracting investors from which functions bitcoin has or does not have, directing attention to irrelevant technicalities and manipulating the bitcoin market. To the best of our knowledge, this perspective has not been thoroughly analysed anywhere else.

A third aim is to propose policy recommendations for governments. Should governments regulate and/or tax bitcoin? If so, how?

1.2 Structure of this book

In this book, we will show that the traditional functions of money have been the same since 9,000 BCE. The main purpose of money is to reduce transaction costs and this requires a stable value (Chapter 3). After describing what bitcoin is (Chapter 2), we analyse whether bitcoin meets those rules and, thus, can be considered money (Chapter 4).

Despite the failure of most ".com" companies after the bursting of the .com bubble, many of these unprofitable companies at least had cash-flow and/or utility, which is a minimum requirement to be considered as an asset. A bitcoin does not have any cash-flow and we will examine if the bitcoin network has any utility. We will also compare bitcoin with gold (Chapter 5). Bitcoin is intangible because it does not exist in physical form. Intangible assets have proven to be valuable. The first such assets were intellectual property, including patents, copyrights. and trademarks. These intangible assets give the owners a competitive advantage in the market. Does bitcoin give the owner a competitive advantage?

Though our conclusion in this book is that bitcoin is not money, not a store of value, not an asset, and does not hedge against anything, the bitcoin network has been extremely successful. The price of a bitcoin has increased from 10 to 30,000 USD in the last nine years. One of the main purposes in this book is to explain the methods that bitcoin promoters use to market and distract potential investors (Chapter 6). They have built a superb brand, used aggressive marketing including co-opting each new bitcoin owner as a newly self-interesting promoter. The promoters have used distraction through visual illusions, nonsense terms, and baffled people with technobabble – constant discussion of irrelevant technology details. Furthermore, we will also explain how a relatively few big owners who own large amounts of bitcoin ("whales") are able to manipulate the bitcoin market and the price movements, thereby cheating the average investor (Chapter 7).

We also analyse how the bitcoin network is *actually* used. The best uses of bitcoin are not something to brag about (Chapter 8). Then, we arrive to the main purpose of the bitcoin network: gambling. Bitcoin, we explain, is unlicensed gambling. To date, existing gambling regulations, including licensing requirements and gambling-specific taxation, that govern other similar forms of gambling have not been enforced against all those operating the bitcoin ecosystem (Chapter 9). We recommend to governments that they enforce their gambling regulations. We finally focus on the waste of electricity and resources by the bitcoin system and why the total social value of the bitcoin system is negative (Chapter 10).

1.3. How we came to follow the advent of bitcoin

Our personal involvement with bitcoin started in 2011 when, at a charity dinner, an entrepreneur started discussing the value of something called "bitcoin. We had never heard of bitcoin. He then explained that bitcoin was a way to print money out of thin air, which, of course, immediately sounded suspicious. He talked about this new digital currency called bitcoin that needed computer power to produce it. He had designed a computer that was specially built to efficiently mint new bitcoin. It was an expensive undertaking, and he needed a short-term loan to mass-produce his computers. Since his specialized computer, he guaranteed, could effectively print money, he would be able pay back the loan in no time at all. He said that the current price of one bitcoin was $10.

Almost everything that sounds too good to be true unfortunately turns out to be too good to be true.

Upon investigation, it looked as if bitcoin might be a Ponzi scheme that would eventually collapse, as all Ponzi schemes eventually do. A Ponzi scheme lures in investors with the promise of high returns. Early investors do well, profiting from funds paid by subsequent investors. With time, it all unravels, and the unsuspecting victims who buy into it late in the game are left proverbially "holding the bag." Charles Dickens describes a similar scheme in his novel, Martin Chuzzlewit, when Martin is taken in by Montague Tigg's unscrupulous insurance business. Ponzi schemes are named after a real-life Charles Ponzi who sold investors on the idea of coupons to replace postage stamps, a similar idea to that of bitcoin replacing money. Readers will remember the more recent Madoff Ponzi scheme. Bernie Madoff died in April 2021 in prison after carrying out a notorious investment swindle.

Our personal entrepreneurial experience in the .com bubble and since has helped reinforce to us that, to make a profit, a company has to have a solid business plan to build the value of its assets. Otherwise, the goal is simply to try to sell your "swamp land in Florida" company shares. You are simply looking for a greater fool who is willing to pay a higher price for the shares than you were initially foolish enough to buy for a high price.

Bitcoin, though not a company share, looked to us, after meeting the entrepreneur in 2011, as if it were also built on the premise of the greater fool theory. Shortly after that meeting, the entrepreneur said that the price of bitcoin fell from $10 to $1, and admitted, very dejectedly, that his plan would no longer work. He was no longer able to guarantee repayment of the loan that he needed. He also believed that, even if the price of bitcoin went back up to $10, there was now a public record of bitcoin's volatility. All bitcoin-related loans would now be hard to obtain and very costly. What happened to this entrepreneur and his specialized computers? Maybe he got out of the bitcoin business. Maybe he kept at it and is now one of the bitcoin billionaires – on paper at least.

Bob Seeman and Roger Svensson

Chapter 2

What is Bitcoin?

B itcoin is considered by many to be a new global form of money. But, as so few of us understand what money is, how can we understand bitcoin? What is money? We understand that we need money to purchase all the items that we have been taught to think that we need in order to be content. However, to really understand the nature of money, we must know something about banking and finance (see Chapter 3). To understand bitcoin, we must understand what the bitcoin innovation actually is.

There are over 4,000 other cryptocurrencies, with mainly similar, but sometimes different characteristics to bitcoin. However, as bitcoin is by far and away the most popular of the cryptocurrencies and has a market value that accounts for approximately 50 percent of the whole crypto market, this book focuses only on bitcoin. You can create your own cryptocurrency (altcoin) in 15 minutes by watching a YouTube video. The following excerpts are from an article published online on April 30, 2020, "How To Create Your Own Cryptocurrency In 15 Minutes - Learn Step-by-Step":

> "… the best and the free method of creating your own cryptocurrency is to use existing open-source code from any existing platform and tweaking it your preferences. This is the method recommended by us and used by many, especially if you are an amateur and don't have a lot of money. This requires very simple coding which you can easily learn…

An altcoin does not start making money right away. It only does so once a substantial amount of community members vouch for it. In order to ensure this for your coin, you have to be acquainted and active within a local crypto community. In fact, you should do this even before you actually make your coin...."

2.1. The mysterious founder of bitcoin

While bitcoin appears to share some of the characteristics of money, it is actually nothing more than a ledger system, a digital spreadsheet that does not significantly differ from other financial record-keeping technology. The bitcoin ledger system uses distributed computing and has some innovative technical features based on cryptography, which, to many people, is intriguing.

What is intriguing as well is the mystery that surrounds the inventor of bitcoin. The inventor's pen name is Satoshi Nakamoto and it is under this name that the original white paper describing bitcoin was published. No one knows who Satoshi Nakamoto is (or, perhaps, was). He may be a man, woman, group of people, or even a government. He registered the bitcoin.org domain name and created a web site for bitcoin in 2008, the year before the circulation of the paper. The vocabulary and English spelling in the Nakamoto paper suggest a British rather than a Japanese background. The Englishness is reinforced by the fact that the paper contains numerous references to the London Times. The hours of the day of internet forum postings from Nakamoto correspond more to the waking hours of Greenwich mean time (United Kingdom time) than to Japanese daytime hours. Numerous individuals have been suspected of being the real bitcoin inventor, but the mystery continues unsolved.

The Nakamoto paper states:

> **"A purely peer-to-peer version of electronic cash would allow online payments to be sent directly from one party to another without going through a financial institution.** Digital

signatures provide part of the solution, but the main benefits are lost if a trusted third party is still required to prevent double-spending. We propose a solution to the double-spending problem using a peer-to-peer network. The network timestamps transactions by hashing them into an ongoing chain of hash-based proof-of-work, forming a record that cannot be changed without redoing the proof-of-work. The longest chain not only serves as proof of the sequence of events witnessed, but proof that it came from the largest pool of CPU power. **As long as a majority of CPU power is controlled by nodes that are not cooperating to attack the network, they'll generate the longest chain and outpace attackers.** [bolding added]"

All that we will focus on in this book is that first above highlighted sentence. The rest of the above paragraph refers to the technical details of implementing the bitcoin network, which are not relevant to this discussion, have been addressed in detail elsewhere, and are easily accessible on the Internet. For some details about the blockchain technology behind bitcoin, you may refer to the sources in the bibliography to this book.

2.2. Irreversible transactions

The goal of Nakamoto was to create a type of payment system that could bypass intermediaries and go directly from purchaser to seller. Payments via digital coins were intended to be not only direct, but also to be anonymous and irreversible.

"Coins" is misleading because no objects are transferred; only the transaction exists. There is not even a transfer of some unique computer data from the seller to the buyer.

All that happens is that the bitcoin accounting ledger is updated. The transaction is a number entry involving a sender and a recipient (both identified only by account numbers), and an amount that is transferred from one to the other. This number entry, or "coin" is meant to be a stand-in for money.

In the bitcoin system, account holders are not required to identify themselves, but that is not unique. Banking systems are based on account numbers, and could, if need be, operate on an anonymous basis, like the storied Swiss bank account. While it is almost always legally necessary for traditional bank account holders to reveal their identity to the bank, this is not technically necessary. Anonymity, therefore, is not a feature that distinguishes bitcoin accounts from traditional bank accounts.

In the real world, when you pay with cash, money goes from your wallet to the seller's, what bitcoin advocates call a "peer-to-peer" transaction. There is no intermediary. But most large modern digital transactions are performed through the good graces of a trusted intermediary. If you pay for a purchase by credit card, the credit card company pays the merchant. You reimburse the credit card company. The credit card company is the trusted intermediary. Likewise, if you pay by debit, the bank is the intermediary since the bank pays the merchants with funds withdrawn from your bank account. Intermediaries can provide a variety of services. For example, the credit card company may reimburse you in cases where the services purchased are not actually provided. However, if you are a merchant who has delivered the goods or services, but the buyer is dissatisfied and the credit card company reverses the payment, you may not be happy with the intermediary. Therefore, there is something to be said for peer-to-peer transactions that are final without intermediaries.

2.3. A single ledger system that avoids manipulation

The bitcoin system keeps a record of all transactions in strict chronological order of occurrence. In the bitcoin system, this record, or ledger, is called a blockchain and is equivalent, in traditional accounting terminology, to a journal. The essential record-keeping mechanism of blockchain, therefore, is no different from ledger books that have been used for hundreds of years, first on stone, then on papyrus, then on paper, then electronically.

Bitcoin uses cryptography (computer secret encoding) to record a transaction between the seller and the buyer. Users typically use a pseudonymous address (like a no-name Swiss bank account number) to identify each other and a passcode (known as a private key) to enter updates into the public ledger (a single publicly available database which one can think of as a single read-only Google® "spreadsheet" common to a vast number of people). This ledger records bitcoin transactions between users. Computers (the "miners" that we will soon discuss) in the bitcoin network validate a transfer, but only one of those computers is able to make the change to the ledger. Through this creative use of technology known as blockchain, bitcoin protects the public ledgers of accounts against manipulation. Users can only "send out" bitcoin that they have electronic access to, permitting validated transactions without the need for a centralized intermediary that both parties trust.

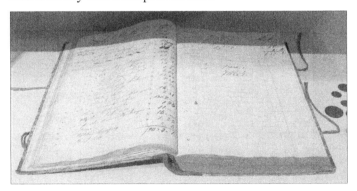

Picture 2.1. A ledger from 1828.
Photographer: Andreas Praefcke

Nakamoto defines a digital coin as a chain of digital signatures. The idea is that all the information needed to validate a transaction is automatically contained within the transaction. This method is a new way to build a ledger, but it does not do away with the need to keep a ledger.

One uniqueness of bitcoin lies in its having a single ledger, distributed across a network of computers, in contrast to traditional bank ledgers kept by each bank in its own centralised computer system. Bitcoin has one single ledger – as does every individual bank.

Multiple synchronised copies of that ledger are distributed across the bitcoin network so that each participant sees the same data. The whole ledger is out in the open for all to see.

The basic principle of a record of transactions and balances recorded by date is no different from what is performed by banks. The concept of a transaction fee as discussed below is also similar to what banks do. The reward of newly minted bitcoin as discussed below is the novel part.

A challenge for the bitcoin system was making certain that miners do not enter fraudulent transactions into the ledger – what Nakamoto referred to as the double-spending problem. Financial institutions avoid double-spending by using a single trusted record keeper, the bank's accounting system, and by periodic audits of the record by third parties. Nakamoto's solution to double-spending was to make the ledger public to all participants, and, by the clever use of cryptography and a complicated algorithm, to make the entry of fraudulent transactions very expensive for anyone who attempts it.

2.4. The miner is the intermediate, who is rewarded

Traditionally, banks have kept track of transactions and managed the financial record-keeping. Nakamoto wanted to bypass banks and outside accountants. Nakamoto refers to the role of banks as one of processing transactions, but banks do more than that. Banks make a legal commitment to convert an account entry into coins, banknotes, general purchasing power money or something else. Banks also provide the payment system and liquidity which enables money to have purchasing power.

With bitcoin, there is no entity that commits to converting the bitcoin into something else and, therefore, the account entry of the bitcoin is meaningless. If a bank (or any other party) were to guarantee to provide liquidity for bitcoin and convert it into money, then the whole idea of it being a direct peer-to-peer network would collapse. The record keeper, the maintainer of the ledger of transactions would then, as it is now, become the bank.

Bitcoin is a system of accounts. It is not a unit of account that passes directly from one owner to another like cash. Also, from a technical perspective, it is not "digital cash" where, for example, a set of unique data goes directly from an App on one party's phone to an App on another party's phone. Instead, with bitcoin, the details of each transaction go from the sender to the single distributed ledger, not from the sender to the recipient. And bitcoin does, despite many claims to the contrary, involve intermediaries. Every bitcoin transaction involves the intermediation of a "miner" as described below.

The operators of the bitcoin network act as their own accountants, called "miners" (as in mining for gold). For each transaction, one mining computer gets to record the transaction in the ledger (make the change in the "spreadsheet") and is rewarded by a transaction fee. This fee is paid in bitcoin, both newly minted bitcoin and bitcoin taken from the bitcoin transaction that the miner has just certified. This is how miners accumulate bitcoin. The transaction fees are variable and change over time. As of May 2021, the average transaction fee was approximately US$ 11 deducted from the amount transferred to which is added a mining reward of 6.25 newly minted bitcoin for each "block" of approximately 500 bitcoin transactions. Each reward translates into a cost to all holders of a bitcoin network since it dilutes the value of the bitcoin they own. It is regularly becoming harder to mine bitcoin and at some point in the future, some estimate 100 years based on the current system, the last bitcoin will be mined and, from then on, only transaction fees will apply.

How the miner who is selected to validate a transaction (the one that gets all the reward) is very interesting. All competitors are presented with a specific complex mathematical problem that can only be solved by brute computing power. Whoever solves the problem first is the winner. From the perspective of an outside observer, the process is random. All miners with the same computing power have an equal chance of solving the problem first. Miners with more computing power have a linearly higher probability of solving the problem first.

The winning miner changes from one transaction to another and is selected through a process that is fair and random. But, nevertheless, there always needs to be such a miner intermediary and all transactions are recorded in a single ledger.

Thus, the winning miner verifies that the same bitcoin is not being spent on more than one transaction (double spending) and sets up a new block (representing approximately the last ten minutes of bitcoin transactions) on the bitcoin blockchain. The other miners, who competed and lost, get nothing. However, all miners in the competition must run their computers and consume electricity (more about this in Chapter 10). Then all the miners immediately move on to the next set of bitcoin transactions that need to be verified.

Initially, miners could not buy anything with their reward money. To get around this problem, Nakamoto implied that miners could advertise their bitcoin rewards received, with the idea that this could generate demand and the public would want to buy their bitcoin for real money. This scheme worked.

As soon as bitcoin units had willing buyers, it became worth their while for miners to mine since mining rewards had become saleable items. Their advertising was initially conducted via websites and social media posts. Now, bitcoin has become a major industry using major marketing channels. Bitcoin is listed on financial exchanges, such as CoinBase and Binance, and is attracting many buyers and sellers. Bitcoin has become an item in demand.

2.5. Summary

The bitcoin system was created by the pseudonym Satoshi Nakamoto in 2008. The original idea was to create a payment system that could go directly between sellers and purchasers, thereby bypassing any intermediaries and avoiding their fees. The system was also to be anonymous and irreversible.

In the bitcoin system, nothing is actually transferred. Only the transactions on different accounts are recorded chronologically in a huge ledger that is visible to everybody. The technology called blockchain protects the public ledger of accounts from being manipulated.

Transactions in the ledger are validated by a vast number of computers in the network controlled by a vast number of different entities. These computers are known as miners, have powerful computing capacity, and compete to solve a complex mathematical problem. After approximately 10 minutes of computing, only the winning miner is rewarded with a transaction fee (deducted from the bitcoin being transferred) and also a number of newly minted bitcoin. A new block is then created. The losing miners get nothing. This process means that there is actually an intermediary that verifies the transaction and there are transaction costs.

Furthermore, although cryptocurrency technology sounds complex, anyone can start their own cryptocurrency within 15 minutes assisted by watching a YouTube video.

Chapter 3

The purpose of money

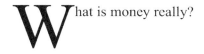What is money really?

3.1. Functions of money

Whether something is money depends on what it does rather than what it is. Any item can be considered as money if it is generally accepted as payment for goods, services, or assets, or as payment of debts, or is a unit of account in a socio-economic context. According to the English economist William Stanley Jevons, for an item to work as "general purpose money", it has to function in the following four ways:

- a medium of exchange;
- a unit of account;
- a store of value; and,
- a standard of deferred payments (credits).

The function as a medium of exchange implies that money is widely acceptable in exchange for goods, services, and assets. Unit of account refers to the relative pricing of goods, services, and assets in terms of the money. Thus, money then reflects the ratio at which various items can be traded. A store of value means that the money retains its value and can be used in future. A standard of deferred payments means that money works as the unit in which postponed payments is undertaken, i.e. it is the function to value debts, thereby allowing goods and services to be acquired now and paid for in the future.

In modern economies, money meets all these functions. However, in many past economies which were not fully monetized, 'special-purpose money' had only one, two or three of these functions.

The ultimate purpose of money is to reduce the transactions costs for payments and credits/loans and to facilitate the relative valuation of goods, services, and assets. Then money works as a lubricant in the economy. A requirement to meet this main purpose is that the item used as money has a stable value.

If the money value is unstable, it will be difficult to make relative valuations of different goods and services as well as to undertake payments and give loans. Money systems also have to be user-friendly, with low risk and low fraud.

Since the invention of money took place long before the human written history, we cannot be sure when and how money first developed. However, livestock, grain, and raw materials for tools (e.g., flint and obsidian) are likely aspirants as the first items to be money and it is believed that this occurred around 9,000 BC when people settled down and became agrarians, according to Glyn Davies. Thereafter, various commodities have been used as money: cacao beans, shells, animal teeth, base metal bracelets and above all, precious metals. Such money is called 'commodity money', where the face value of money is very close to the intrinsic value of the commodity. Thus, the money carries its value in it. This is contrast to 'fiat money', which has no (or low) intrinsic value and where the money value is not determined by the raw material value of the commodity but by the issuer's, generally now a government, credibility or economy.

How well a commodity works as commodity money depends on how its characteristics meet the functions of money. Food has obviously a limited function as a store of value as it will rot or be eaten by pests. Other items like shells and animal teeth are more durable but can be rare in some areas and extremely abundant in others. Furthermore, they are seldom standardized.

Precious metals (particularly gold and silver) best meet the requirements of commodity money, since they have some extraordinary characteristics. Precious metals: 1) are resistant to corrosion and oxidation; 2) exist in limited quantities; 3) are well known; and 4) are relatively soft. Thanks to these desirable characteristics, precious metals received an exchange value and were used as money. Money using such metals then became durable (non-corroding), received a stable value (limited but known quantity), portable (a high value compared with their size), of a size that could be stored easily (a high value compared with their size), and easy to process and to divide in small pieces (soft metal). Thus, the high value of gold and silver is not based on their technological or industrial characteristics, but rather on their function as a store of value and exchange value when bartering with other goods and services. In many parts of the world, people discovered early that gold and silver were the most precious metal, not least evidenced by its presence in treasure finds (Picture 3.1).

Picture 3.1. Hoard of British medieval gold coins.

3.2. Coins as standardized money

A further step in the history of money was standardization. A coin is a piece of hard material of standardized weight and fineness, which are guaranteed/controlled by an authority with a hallmark. Usually, coins are made of precious metals.

The face value of coins is higher than their intrinsic value in areas where the coins are legal tender for two reasons:

- Lower transaction costs: When conducting daily (small) transactions, it is easier to count coins than to weigh and ascertain the fineness of silver. Thus, the transaction costs are lowered. This practice implies that the medium of exchange and unit of account functions are better performed by coins than by un-minted metal. Therefore, people are generally willing to pay a premium to have their silver transformed into standard coins. With standardized coins, more people who neither had the ability to ascertain fineness nor had scales, could participate in market activities.
- Network effects: Coins are also a typical network good. That is, the value of holding coins increases as more people accept coins as a medium of exchange and a standard of value, which reinforces and tends to increase the premium. This network characteristic is crucial when explaining why certain coins become international standards of payment.

The premium component enables the coin-issuing authority to generate profits from minting (seignorage). In practice, it is the agents in the market who determine the level of this premium component, i.e., how much more valuable it is to hold coins than un-minted metal. The usage of coins instead of unstandardized precious metals means that people must trust the authority or institution which guarantees the fineness and weight. The authority has the role of monitoring/supervising the monetary system and detecting counterfeiting. History has shown that all standardized money has been issued by an authority, while non-standardized money in pre-history were not issued by an authority.

The first coins were minted in Lydia, India and China in the late 7th and early 6th centuries BC. The Lydian coins were made of electrum, a natural alloy of gold and silver, and standardized with respect to fineness and weight.

They had a stamped design on the obverse and an incused punch mark on the reverse. The practice of minting standardized coins then spread rapidly throughout the Greek world.

In Antiquity, the Middle Ages, and the early modern period (1500–1800), precious metals – especially gold and silver – have been the main raw material of commodity money. Copper and bronze have occasionally been used for small coin denominations.

A recurring problem with coins as commodity money has been coin debasements. In times when governments' finances were in disarray due to wars or epidemics, debasements through lowering the fineness – by inserting base metals – have been used as a solution to increase the government incomes. Empirical observations do show that such debasements increased the revenues for the king/issuer in the short run but caused inflation and re-distribution of income and wealth between groups in the society. Above all, debasements undermined confidence in the monetary system and caused severe damage to both economy and trade in terms of higher transactions costs and uncertainty.

One of the main costs of commodity money is that valuable precious metals such as gold and silver are bound to the monetary system and do not earn any interest rate. A first step was to issue banknotes as receipts for deposits. These banknotes began circulating as money in place of the deposited coins. Part of the deposited precious metals could then be lent and earn an interest rate. This occurred in the 1660s in Sweden and in the 1710s in France. In both cases, the consequence was over-issuance of banknotes causing bank-runs, financial chaos, and ruined holders of banknotes. After this, people were skeptical of banknotes.

But as time went by, many countries again started issuing banknotes backed by gold. The gold standard was settled in the 19th century with the United Kingdom and the United States as leading countries. Since not all banknotes were backed by gold, part of the monetary stock could be considered as fiat money. During the World War I, the gold standard system broke down due to over-issuance of money. Chaotic scenes with hyper-inflation followed in the 1920s, especially among Central European countries that had lost the war. A new attempt with a gold standard started in the mid-1920s in many countries but was abandoned in 1931 after speculative attacks against currencies. After World War II, the international Bretton Wood system was created as a kind of gold standard. The US dollar was pegged to gold. The Federal Reserve promised to convert 35 US dollars to 1 oz of gold, and other countries pegged their currencies to the dollar.

3.3. Towards a pure fiat money system

When the Bretton Woods-system broke down in 1971, a pure global fiat money system emerged for the first time in history. The biggest advantage with such a system is that no precious metals at all needed to be bound to the monetary system. Such metals can instead be used as a store of value, collateral or be sold for cash which can be lent and earn an interest rate. The largest risk with a pure fiat money system is that there is no limit how much money can be "printed", since the intrinsic value is close to zero. In contrast, the stored precious metals set a limit on money issuing in a commodity money system.

In almost all modern-day economies, money is provided through a public-private partnership between a government central bank and private banks. Electronic bank deposits are the main means for trade among bank customers, while going through the central bank are the means of payment between banks. Although electronic money dominates today, physical money in the form of banknotes and coins still circulates (Picture 3.2). The two-tier system is generally trustworthy because it is carefully regulated and monitored. The central bank has the task to ensure that everything operates as it should and that liquidity of money is high, i.e., that citizens can be sure that money exchanges are smooth equitable and prompt.

Picture 3.2. Fiat money banknotes from the 20th century.

Money in such a dual fiat system can either be created by the central bank through open market operations and lending to commercial banks or by commercial banks through lending to firms and households. Since the history from 1971 has shown that money supply and inflation can easily accelerate in a fiat money system, the main task of government central banks is to maintain price stability and the value of the domestic currency. Here, the central bank has three main instruments: open market operations, bank reserve requirement and interest rate policy:

- Open market operations implies that the central bank through buying and selling of various financial instruments – primarily government bonds – manages the quantity of money into circulation and affects market interest rates.
- Through the bank reserve requirement, the central bank sets the minimum amounts of reserves that must be held by a commercial bank. The level of this requirement affects the amount of funds available for commercial banks to make loans with, and, thus, indirectly the monetary base.
- The central bank can increase or decrease the interest rate it charges on loans from the central

bank to commercial banks (discounts or overdrafts). The interest rate will affect the credit available in the economy.

Theoretically, central banks are seen as independent authorities of their governments. However, in practice, they are not. If a government runs huge deficits, it has to raise funds through issuing of bonds or short terms interest-bearing assets. Issuing many such financial assets will cause both the market interest rate and inflation to raise. In such case, the central bank needs to buy these bonds in open market operations which expands money supply, and there is a risk with a negative spiral of both expanding money supply and inflation. Therefore, a stable currency value is closely linked to stable finances of the government and that the government can meet its financial obligations.

Other roles of the central bank are to ensure financial stability, i.e. acting as the bankers' bank, to manage a country's reserves of foreign-exchange, gold reserves and government bonds, to regulate and supervise the banking industry, and to issue physical banknotes and coins.

Even if today's monetary system is based on fiat money, money still has the four functions as stated above, and the main purpose is to reduce transactions costs for payments and loans as well as relative valuations. This requires a stable money value.

3.4. International currencies

The network effect of money has led to a situation that fewer and not more currencies have been used as international currencies in world trade over the history of money. Often, a specific currency has had a predominant position. According to the American professor in economics, Barry Eichengreen, at least four basic requirements must be met for a currency to function as a dominant international currency:

- The currency must have a long-term stable value.

- The currency must be in sufficient volume to meet the needs of international trade in goods, services, and financial assets.
- It must be possible to make transactions at low costs. Differences between bid and ask prices must be small and liquidity high.
- There must be a trusted issuer who is military, financially and politically stable enough to guarantee the currency.

Based on these terms, market participants choose which currency should be the most viable in world trade. No supranational authority is needed.

The terms apply regardless of whether it is about commodity money or fiat money.

For fiat money, it is particularly important to have an issuer, as the currency implies a debt or a commitment to the holder.

All the currencies that have historically functioned as dominant international currencies for a longer period of time meet the above four requirements. These are Athenian tetradrachms (c. 480–150 BC), Roman denarii (210 BC–190 AD), Byzantine solidus (300–1035) (Picture 3.3), florins and ducats from Florence and Venice (1250–1600), Dutch guilder and ducats (1600–1780), British pounds (1800–1918), and finally US dollars (1918–present).

Picture 3.3. The Byzantine gold coin solidus is the most long-lived international currency in history. Content and weight were unchanged for more than 700 years. Solidus issued by Emperor Constantius II (355–61), 20 mm and 4.49 g.

3.5. Summary

Money has four functions: 1) a medium of exchange; 2) a unit of account; 3) a store of value and 4) a standard of deferred payments. The ultimate purpose of money is to reduce transaction costs for payments and loans and to facilitate relative valuations. This requires a stable value of the money. Many different items have been used as commodity money, but precious metals, with gold being the very best, have the preferred characteristics to fulfil the functions of money. These characteristics made them valuable. Gold is non-corroding, exists in limited volumes, is well-known and is a soft metal that is easy to process. When standardized money in the form of coins were introduced, transactions costs were further reduced. Then, an authority was needed to guarantee and monitor the system.

Since 1971, the world has had a pure fiat money system. Such a system depends on people trusting that the issuing countries can meet their financial obligations. The central banks have a high responsibility to maintain a stable value of the currencies and to provide liquidity to the financial system. Thus, the main four functions and purpose of money are still valid today as they were in Antiquity and the Middle Ages. The network characteristics of money imply that a specific currency has often been predominant in international trade in history. Such a currency must have a stable value, be issued in large volumes, have low transaction costs, and have a stable issuer.

Chapter 4

Is bitcoin money?

B itcoin has been marketed as the money of the future. Bitcoin is built on the idea of excluding third-party intermediaries, enabling individuals to make transactions directly with other individuals. But how well does bitcoin meet the functions and requirements of money?

4.1. Unpredictable and volatile value

As we concluded in the previous chapter, in order for money to reduce transactions costs for payments, loans and relative valuations, it must have a stable value. When it comes to regular currencies, a central authority, e.g. the central bank, adjusts the value of money according to need, even when it means absorbing a loss. By contrast, in a decentralized network of bitcoin users, there is no central agent who has an obligation or, indeed, the incentive, to stabilize the value of bitcoin. As a consequence, the value of bitcoin will fluctuate whenever demand increases or decreases. The history of bitcoin shows that its value fluctuates unpredictably.

Figure 4.1. Prices of bitcoin in US dollars, June 2015 - June 2021, monthly data.

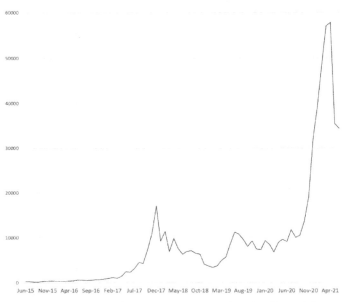

Source: Svensson (2021). Data processed and collected from various sources.

From January to December 2017 the price made an approximate 20-fold increase from 900 to 17,000 USD. A major crash occurred from December 2017 to June 2018 when the price dropped from about 20,000 to 6,000 USD. The price of bitcoin then varied between 3,000 and 10,000 USD until August 2020. Once again, there was a huge increase in the price from August 2020 to mid-March 2021 from 10,000 to 60,000 USD. On March 24, 2021 Elon Musk tweeted that anyone could use bitcoin as payment for Tesla cars. Later, on May 12, Musk withdrew this opportunity. Within a couple of months, the value halved to less than 30,000 USD (June 23). The values of other cryptocurrencies have varied even more sharply (see, for example, ethereum in Figure 4.2 which figure uses an index = 100 as of January 1, 2017).

Figure 4.2. Volatility of bitcoin (BTC) and ethereum (ETH)
June 2015 - June 2021, *index=100 as of January 1, 2017,*
monthly data.

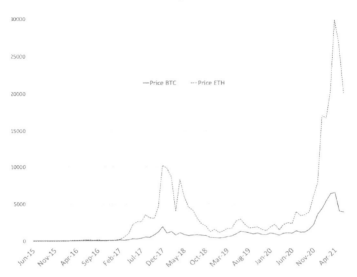

Source: Roger Svensson (2021). Data processed and collected
from various sources.

During the spring and summer of 2021, it has been common for the bitcoin price to have varied ten percent up or down in a single day. In practice, this means a variation of between 3,000 and 6,000 USD per bitcoin per day. It is true that fiat currencies in a spiral of hyperinflation have had significantly higher depreciation than ten percent per day, but in such cases the movements have been monotonous in one direction: down.

Such a high volatility in the value of bitcoin implies that bitcoin is a bad store of value. It is not only the volatility that causes problems as a store of value, but also the unpredictable movements in price that is affected by one or a few famous individuals that make a public comment on bitcoin.

One day you can buy a Tesla for a bitcoin, another day a Kia.

A conclusion from this section is that bitcoin does not fulfill the basic requirement of a currency: a stable value.

4.2. Does not meet any function of money

Based on the analysis in the previous section, bitcoin is obviously a bad store of value. This fact makes it almost impossible to use bitcoin as a standard of deferred payments (loans) or as a unit of account. If the value of an item can go up or down by ten percent a day, it becomes extremely difficult to arrange a loan in terms of such an item.

Unit of account

Currently, in contrast to much of the content of its widespread advertisement campaign, and despite the fact that it is widely traded, bitcoin is not publicly used anywhere as a unit of account. It is not used for pricing or invoicing. Wages are not measured in bitcoins. Taxes are not measured in bitcoin, and government do not accept bitcoin as a legal tender or for payments (recent exception: see El Salvador below). Further, no legitimate company or government prices their good or services in bitcoin. Even *conferences about bitcoin* price their conference fees in real currencies because the price volatility could wipe out their profit margins overnight. Bitcoin is, rather, an accounting system for a possible digital asset (more about this in Chapter 5).

Transaction costs

On June 9, 2021, El Salvador became the first country in the world to adopt bitcoin as a legal tender after Congress approved a proposal of President Bukele. The plan is that bitcoin will become a legal tender within 90 days (September 7). Since El Salvador lacks its own currency, bitcoin will work as a legal tender alongside the US dollar, which has been the only legal tender from 2001 until today. Prices may then be expressed, and taxes paid, in bitcoin. The President's idea is that bitcoin has a potential to help Salvadorans living abroad to send remittances home. He also thinks that volcanic energy can be used for bitcoin mining. Unsurprisingly, bitcoin enthusiasts around the world became lyrical of the announcement. One has to remember that only 30 percent of adults in El Salvador have a bank account, and the finances of the government are in disarray. Therefore, the decision by the Congress appears more like a panic measure. Furthermore, all scientific knowledge about how bitcoin works as a medium of exchange predicts that this attempt will be a big failure.

As a medium of exchange, the transaction costs of bitcoin are high. These costs consist not only of the fee for the transaction but also the time (see below) it takes to get the transaction verified. Because the average transaction fee was 11 USD as of May 2021, the system favors larger transactions. It is therefore completely improbable that bitcoin transactions will ever become commonplace for small everyday transactions.

Bitcoin is much more catastrophic in terms of the time-cost of transactions. The capacity ceiling in the bitcoin system is six or seven transactions per second, while the VISA® network can conduct 65,000 transactions per second. While VISA can verify a transaction in a fraction of one second, it can currently take about ten minutes for a bitcoin transaction to be verified. This delay is very bad for retail transactions. And the more people that use the bitcoin system, the longer the wait. In order to limit the number of transactions added to the ledger at any given time (see Chapter 2), new blocks in the blockchain can only be added at pre-specified intervals. However, because there is a limit to the number of transactions in any block, this creates a queue, causing bottlenecks. If the use of bitcoin for real world transactions is significantly expanded, bottlenecks would be severe. It is not unlikely that a transaction would take hours or even days to be verified. Thus, the bitcoin network does not scale with increasing volume – the transaction fee is fixed, and the waiting time, under the current bitcoin system, will become exponential.

Some believe that bitcoin provides access to markets to individuals in the developing world who are not well served by banks or central financial institutions. Many people without bank accounts in developing countries have to rely on expensive international money transfers such as Western Union. In such cases, bitcoin transfers could be an alternative. However, the recipients must immediately exchange their bitcoins into the local currency or the US dollar, and many do not have the necessary technology available for this exchange. As time goes by and financial institutions develop in poor countries, both Western Union services and bitcoin transfers will disappear.

As explained in Chapter 2, credit card transactions are reversible, whereas, with bitcoin, once made, are final. Finality has many advantages but, in cases of fraud, it should be possible to reverse a transaction. Even if reversal were technically possible, with bitcoin, there is no trusted intermediary that can make the determination of fraud.

A conclusion from this section is that bitcoin does not fulfil the main purpose of money – to reduce transactions costs for payments and loans and to facilitate relative valuation of products and assets. Rather it is the opposite – transaction costs are huge.

4.3. Will never become an international currency

Many have proposed that bitcoin will take over as an international currency in the future. A closer examination shows that bitcoin would never work as an international currency. None of the four conditions in section 3.4 are met for bitcoin. First, bitcoin has greater volatility than any other currency in history. Price changes of tens of percent up or down within a couple of days are commonplace. Second, there is a predetermined maximum amount of bitcoin (21 million) that can be created. With a current market value of approximately 30,000 USD, this implies a total value of 630 billion USD, which cannot satisfy the needs of international trade. If bitcoin is to cover these needs, the relative value of the currency must increase, which would make its price even more unstable. Some bitcoin promoters say that *since* bitcoin *will* be the international currency, the price of bitcoin will have to increase in value to $X million in order to satisfy the needs of international trade. That "since" is a huge assumption.

In fact, the number of bitcoin transactions has never exceeded 10 million per month during the last ten years. This means around four transactions per second (as a month has approximately 2.6 million seconds), close to the current six or seven transactions per second ceiling. However, the designers and operators (miners) of the bitcoin network will likely revise the software protocol to raise the ceiling when needed. Third, transaction costs are high since it takes a long time to complete transactions. Last, but not least, there is no stable issuer that can guarantee the currency or meet any obligations. If one or more jurisdictions were to ban, or effectively ban, transactions with, or possession of, bitcoin, the fairy tale may soon be over. China is the leading country moving in this direction.

4.4. Even bad as token money

In monetary history, there has often been a shortage of small denominations as long as the coinage system has been full-bodied, i.e., all denominations have proportional intrinsic values compared to their face values. The explanation is the higher costs to produce small change – all production steps, like engraving dies, preparing blanks, and striking coins are as time consuming for small as for large coins. These higher costs meant that few government authorities were willing to issue small change.

Since small change was required for daily transactions, a big problem arose. Historically, the market solved this problem by issuing so called "token coins" made by base metals. These were used as small change and often convertible to a currency or commodities by the issuer. First, token money is not issued by a central authority, but instead by cities or private firms. Second, it always has a face value far above its intrinsic value. Third, token money has a limited legal tender. Usually, it is valid for payments within restricted geographical areas and is not accepted for tax payments. The issuing of token money could be sanctioned or not by the government authority. However, since governments often were aware that token money solved the problem of shortage of small change, they did not discourage its issuance.

Bitcoin qualifies as token money on all three points above. Bitcoin has a decentralized issuance, has a face value far above its intrinsic value and is only accepted as a medium of exchange among a limited number of persons (among a subset of those who believe that bitcoin has a value). However, in contrast to the token coins – issued by decentralized cities and firms – that met a function as small change alongside the legal tender, bitcoin has hardly any function as money alongside the legal tender currencies (exceptions: among criminals and for money laundering, see next section). Furthermore, there is no issuer that takes the responsibility to convert bitcoin into a currency or a commodity if something goes wrong with the system.

In summary, bitcoin and other cryptocurrencies are not the first decentralized system of issuance of standardized money. Such systems occurred several hundred years ago as token coins issued by thousands of independent firms and cities.

4.5. Legitimate and fake trade, and illegitimate payments

Almost all bitcoin transactions are simply trading in bitcoin, i.e., the buying and selling of bitcoin as a kind of asset. For such trades, bitcoin is not being used as a means of payment. Trading of bitcoin is both real trading and fake trades. Research in 2019 claimed that 95% of the reported volume of trades was fake (see Chapters 7 and 8). The balance of 5% was for both legitimate trades and also actual purchases of goods and services. Since then, legitimate trading has vastly increased, and regulatory enforcement has likely reduced fake trading. However, for the purposes of this rough calculation, we will assume that these two trading volume changes roughly balance each other out so the percentage changes will be ignored (there is no current publicly available data.) Further, in January 2020, The New York Times reported that one percent of all bitcoin transactions was for illicit activity such as money laundering, payments for illegal goods or services, thefts of bitcoin, and ransomware payments. Therefore, a back-of-the-envelope estimate is that legitimate trading and legitimate purchases make up the remaining the balance of 4% of all bitcoin transactions. Based on all the advertising about buying and selling bitcoin, a conservative estimate is that there are (and also were in 2019 and 2020) at least 10 times as many legitimate trades as legitimate purchases. This rough analysis leads to the result that a fraction of 1% of all bitcoin transactions are for legitimate purchases. As 1% of all transactions have been identified as being used for crime, this rough analysis indicates that there are significantly more illegitimate purchases using bitcoin than legitimate purchases. As a means of payment, bitcoin is mainly used for illegitimate purposes. In January 2021, Treasury Secretary Janet Yellen agreed, stating: "I think many [cryptocurrencies] are used, at least in a [purchase] sense, mainly for illicit financing."

Criminals find bitcoin attractive because transactions using bitcoin or other similar cryptocurrency can help to circumvent the traditional criminal transaction and anti-money laundering checks conducted by financial institutions. Transactions with bitcoin are not anonymous as explained in Chapter 2, but buyers and sellers are anonymous to each other (referred to as second party anonymity). Bitcoin transactions do not require people to use their real names, nor are there true bank account numbers, which is a bonanza for criminals. Their bitcoin addresses (wallets) are pseudonyms.

Bitcoin's second-party anonymity has some benefits for criminals, including tax evasion, terrorist financing, gun smuggling, human trafficking, and money laundering. Many online stores dealing in illegal goods do accept bitcoin as payment. Further, after their ransomware attacks, cyber-attackers also accept bitcoin as a ransom payment for people to regain access to their computer system. The rare company, and even rarer government, accepts bitcoin as payment and almost all of those, after receiving the bitcoin, quickly sell the bitcoin to obtain real currencies.

In the more traditional money laundering world, laundering can be performed by purchasing gold bars, cars, jewellery, or real estate with the funds derived from criminal activities, and then later reselling these assets on the open market. Using bitcoin makes laundering more convenient, especially across international borders. It can be performed online with no need to first buy gold bars, yachts, or expensive homes. This makes it harder for law enforcement, regulators, and compliance departments at financial institutions to identify illicit transactions and to trace origins and destinations. See Appendix B, a U.S. Justice Department press release regarding money laundering and bitcoin.

However, the FBI's success in tracking and retrieving part of the bitcoin ransom paid to the cyberattacker collective DarkSide in the ransom attack against Colonial Pipeline raised public awareness of the fact that bitcoin transactions are traceable and not anonymous to the government. There is more about this in Chapter 8 about regulation.

4.6. Summary

As money, bitcoin is almost useless. Its extremely unpredictable and volatile value implies that it can neither function as a store value, a unit of account nor a standard of deferred payments. The only function might be as a medium of exchange, but the limited capacity of the blockchain system makes transactions costs high in terms of waiting time. If more people would use bitcoin for transactions than today, bottlenecks would be huge. Thus, bitcoin does not even fulfil the main purpose of money – to reduce transaction costs for payments, loans, and relative valuations. The unpredictable value, the small volume and high transactions costs also disqualify bitcoin as an international currency.

Because bitcoin is not issued by a central government, has a limited legal tender and a face value far above its intrinsic value, it is similar to token money. Unlike the historical token coins that had a function as small change and were convertible into a currency or a commodity, bitcoin lacks both of these features. Historical records show that a decentralized monetary system with tokens existed several hundred years ago. Therefore, even the claim that bitcoin is the first decentralized money system is false.

Statistics show that almost all transactions with bitcoin are simply trades. Illegitimate purchases account for approximately 1% of all transactions and legitimate purchases a fraction of 1%. The popularity of bitcoin among criminals and money launderers is linked to the increased ability to bypass anti-money laundering checks in the financial system. However even then, in many cases, governments can trace bitcoin transactions to the person owning the wallet.

In summary, we can rule out any claims that bitcoin has any function as regular money. Therefore, in the next chapter, we turn to the question of whether bitcoin is an asset.

Chapter 5
Not even an asset

An asset is any resource (tangible or intangible) that can be used to produce a positive economic value. The owner of the asset can convert the asset into cash or obtain a monetary value from it. This ability to convert means that the monetary value of the asset can be used in the balance sheet of the owner.

Both tangible and intangible assets have some kind of cash flow or utility that generates revenues. For example, stocks provide dividends, bonds pay coupons and loans give interest. The present value of the future cash flows is then used to determine the fundamental value of the asset. Furthermore, real estate provides rents or housing services that can be used to determine the value of the asset. Other assets like silver, copper, oil, or gas can be used directly as commodities, inputs to produce other commodities, or energy. Intangible assets like software, goodwill, patents, copyrights, and trademarks have a value because they give the owners a competitive advantage in the market.

Assets can be used as collateral or mortgage on loans. The volatility of the asset value and the liquidity of the asset, i.e. how easily it is converted into cash, determine how well it works as collateral or mortgage.

5.1. Does bitcoin qualify as an asset?

Bitcoin is, in its nature, non-physical and intangible. The bitcoin system is an accounting system for a digital item. But does it provide any cash flow or utility? Obviously, bitcoin does not provide any cash flow in terms of dividends or coupons. It does not provide any housing services, rents or other services as real estate does. It cannot be used as a commodity, an input for a commodity, or as energy. Furthermore, bitcoin does not give any competitive advantage whatsoever in the market – as intellectual property does – for the owner. Thus, bitcoin provides no cash flow or utility, has no intrinsic value at all, and it is not backed by anything. Because there is no cash flow or utility, no method to calculate the fundamental value of bitcoin exists.

As we saw in section 4.5, the bitcoin system is used by criminals for money laundering and for transferring gains from criminal activities. However, this usage is marginal and accounts for only approximately 1 percent of all transactions. Further, of course, governments around the world are trying to stop such illegal use.

However, as explained in "How to Get a Bitcoin (BTC) Loan" by SoFi in December 2020, bitcoin is being used as collateral for loans on various bitcoin platforms, but not in the ordinary financial sector.

5.2. Comparison with gold

Fidelity Digital Assets, a professional Wall Street investment firm, published a report entitled "Bitcoin Investment Thesis, Bitcoin's Role as an Alternative Investment" dated October 2020. It states in part:

> "The careful and informed use of alternative investments in a diversified portfolio can reduce risk, lower volatility, and improve returns over the long-term, enhancing investors' ability to meet their return outcomes."

> "Modern Portfolio Theory (MPT) argues that investors can design a diversified portfolio of investments that generates maximum returns while minimizing unsystematic risk."

> "One of the key reasons for including alternatives in a portfolio is to increase diversification by allocating to assets or investments that are driven by different risk and return factors relative to traditional investments and are thus imperfectly correlated. The inclusion of assets that are

imperfectly correlated may offer downside protection when traditional assets fall and may help reduce volatility. Diversification can lower risk without necessarily causing an offsetting reduction in expected return and is therefore generally viewed as a highly desirable method of generating improved risk-adjusted returns."

Thus, an asset that is negatively correlated with most other assets such as real estate and shares would be ideal to include in a diversified portfolio. Such an asset would be highly demanded. As depicted in Figure 5.1, history has shown that gold is such an asset with negative correlation to shares. Since 1971 when the US dollar lost its pegging at 35 USD per troy ounce, gold has systematically had a return negatively correlated to that of the Standard & Poor 500 index. The correlation between the annual returns in Figure 5.1 is - 0.22. In fact, throughout history, gold has been seen as a safe store of value all over the world, especially during crises and turbulent periods (see for example Klein et al. 2018). But the gold price also rises with inflation and inflation expectations. Therefore, gold is regarded as, perhaps, the best inflation hedge.

It should be noted that gold does not generate any cash flow, and its use in industry is highly limited as compared to other precious metals such as silver and copper. In addition, gold has no issuer, although standardized gold pieces can be stamped and guaranteed by authorities. In Chapter 3, we explained why gold has been in such demand throughout history. It is the best-known store of value, exists in limited quantities (only a total of 200,000 tons world-wide), is well-known world-wide, and is easy to process and to use as jewelry or coins.

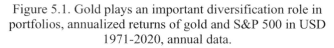

Figure 5.1. Gold plays an important diversification role in portfolios, annualized returns of gold and S&P 500 in USD 1971-2020, annual data.

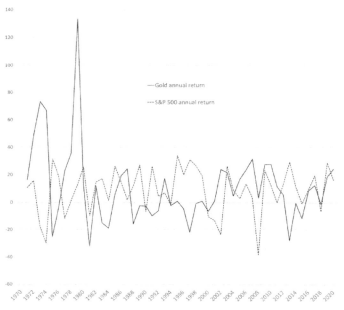

Source of data: macrotrends.net, summarized by Roger Svensson.

Bitcoin has been marketed as "the digital gold" and many have claimed that bitcoin will replace gold as a safe asset in diversified portfolios. In section 4.1, however, we showed statistically how volatile bitcoin and other cryptocurrencies are. And a closer examination undertaken by Goldman Sachs (Global Macro Research Issue 98), where the bitcoin price volatility is compared to the volatility of real asset prices such as oil, silver, S&P 500 index or bonds does not provide a better result. For example, bitcoin has twice the daily volatility than the most volatile real asset, oil. Therefore, bitcoin represents anything but a low-risk asset. The ceiling of 21 million bitcoin issued has never helped it as a stable store of value or as a low-risk item to hold. Furthermore, there is nothing in the relatively short history of bitcoin that indicates that bitcoin would be negatively correlated with, for example, shares (see for example Klein et al. 2018). As noted by

Nouriel Roubini, when US stock markets fell approximately 35 percent in the spring of 2020, bitcoin fell by 50 percent and other cryptocurrencies dropped even more. This correlation indicates that bitcoin is, instead, pro-cyclical. In July 2020, researchers Thomas Conlon and Richard McGee concluded:

> "The Covid-19 bear market presents the first acute market losses since active trading of Bitcoin began. This market downturn provides a timely test of the frequently expounded safe haven properties of Bitcoin. In this paper, we show that Bitcoin does not act as a safe haven, instead decreasing in price in lockstep with the S&P 500 as the crisis develops. When held alongside the S&P 500, even a small allocation to Bitcoin substantially increases portfolio downside risk. Our empirical findings cast doubt on the ability of Bitcoin to provide shelter from turbulence in traditional markets."

Another problem with bitcoin is that it can disappear any time when another digital item turns up that has better and more desirable features, or if the bitcoin system – without any responsible authority – technically breaks down for any reason. In contrast, gold will not disappear. Metallurgists have been trying for 6,000 years to create real gold in an artificial way or an alloy with better features than gold. All have failed.

5.3. No hedge against regular currency depreciation

Many claim that the value of bitcoin comes from scarcity since there is an absolute ceiling of 21 million bitcoin that can be issued. However, scarcity in itself creates no value. To create something that is rare in an artificial way is not difficult at all. Furthermore, there is no limit to how many different types of cryptocurrencies can be created. Today, we already have more than 4,000 of them, and the number increases every day. In addition, many of the cryptocurrencies, such as ethereum and dogecoin, do not have a maximum supply of how many of them can be created.

A recurrent argument for holding bitcoin and other cryptocurrencies is the depreciation, and expectations of higher depreciation in the future, of the fiat currencies, with the US dollar at the forefront. Since the global financial crisis in 2007-09, money supply of the fiat currencies has increased significantly. However, this has not been mirrored in inflation of the consumer price indices. The reason is that money supply has mainly expanded through credits. Loans need collateral and, therefore, borrowers have invested their money in assets. Thus, the large increase in money supply has caused an asset inflation as well as a higher debt-ratio in the private sector. But sooner or later the asset inflation may spillover on prices in the consumption sector. Recently (spring 2021), the annual inflation rate increased to five percent in the United States. Many claim that this is transitory, but who knows how to stop a snowball that has started rolling? The authors of this book will not defend the central banks' heavy expansion of money supply during the last 10 - 15 years. However, the risk of fiat money depreciation is not a reason that resources should be used to buy bitcoin or other cryptocurrencies. To buy bitcoin for this reason is like jumping out of the frying pan and into the fire.

Nouriel Roubini points out in a Goldman Sachs report that the tenfold rise in the bitcoin price from 6,000 to 60,000 USD in one year (between March 2020 and March 2021) cannot be explained by a fear of a high depreciation of the USD and other fiat currencies. In such case, the traditional inflation hedge, gold, would have increased far more than it has. Finally, within a couple of weeks this spring, as well as in 2018, the bitcoin price fell 50 percent, which is unmatched by any of the major fiat currencies in the last 50 years since the collapse of Bretton Woods.

5.4. Only gambling remains

At this point of the analysis, we have concluded that bitcoin neither functions as money nor as an asset. Furthermore, it will not replace gold as a safe store of value in a crisis and it is no hedge against fiat currency depreciation. These conclusions mean that only one alternative for bitcoin remains.

A financial bubble occurs when an asset is valued far above its fundamental value. But in the case of bitcoin, no fundamental value can be calculated at all since bitcoin does not provide any cash flow or utility. Based on the analysis in the previous and the present chapters, the huge ups and downs in the bitcoin price can only be explained by speculative gambling. Bitcoin seems to be traded for speculative purposes and that the traders rely on the greater fool theory. They try to find someone else who is willing to pay more for it. A critical part of bitcoin is trust that other people consider bitcoin valuable to hold. We will write more about bitcoin as gambling in Chapter 9.

5.5. Summary

Tangible and intangible assets have cash flow or utility that produce positive economic value. The present value of the cash flow and utility can be used to calculate the fundamental value of the asset. This principle applies for all assets including shares, real estate, bonds, and intellectual property. Bitcoin provides neither any cash flow nor utility. Thus, no fundamental value can be estimated for bitcoin. Bitcoin simply lacks an intrinsic value.

An asset that is negatively correlated with most other assets such as real estate and shares would be ideal to include in a diversified portfolio. Historically, gold has had this role. It is regarded as among the safest investments in a crisis and is an excellent inflation hedge. Although gold neither generates any cash flow, it has other desirable features as a hedge mentioned above and as the best-known store of value. The claim that bitcoin is "the digital gold" and will replace gold as a portfolio diversifier lacks any scientific evidence. The high volatility of bitcoin and its pro-cyclical price movements rule this out.

The argument that scarcity creates value is nonsense. To create something that is rare in an artificial way is not difficult at all. Anyway, today, there are already 4,000 cryptocurrencies, and more coming all the time. Furthermore, there is no responsible issuer. So, if the bitcoin system breaks down, holders have nobody from whom to claim – or to whom to assign blame.

A final argument is that bitcoin is a hedge against the fear of depreciation of fiat currencies. Although the behavior of many central banks – expanding money supply heavily over the last 15 years – is difficult to defend, this does not imply that cryptocurrencies are the alternative. The 50 percent depreciation of bitcoin in the spring 2018 and 2021 is unmatched by any of the main fiat currencies in the last 50 years. Therefore, our conclusion is that the large ups and downs in the bitcoin price depend on speculative gambling and rely on the greater fool theory.

Bob Seeman and Roger Svensson

Chapter 6

Deception through distraction

I n the previous chapters, we have concluded that:

- Bitcoin is very bad money, since the high volatility of its price makes it useless as a store of value, as a unit of account and as a standard of deferred payment. Furthermore, high transaction costs (especially regarding time) hinder bitcoin as a medium of exchange. The ultimate purpose of money is to reduce transaction costs for payments, loans, and valuations, not to increase them (as bitcoin does).
- Bitcoin does not have any cash flow or utility, implying that no fundamental value of bitcoin can be calculated. Thus, it is not an asset and has no intrinsic value.
- Bitcoin is not a hedge against inflation and does not have a value that is negatively correlated with real assets such as shares and real estate.
- The main purpose of bitcoin is speculative gambling.

Nevertheless, bitcoin has been extremely successful by increasing in value from 10 to approximately 30,000 USD from August 2012 to June 2021 – a 3,000-fold increase in less than nine years. In this chapter, we are going to explain which kinds of methods the promoters behind bitcoin use to market the bitcoin system and distract potential investors and miners from the reality and scientific facts. One obvious method is the manipulating of orders, trade, and prices of bitcoin, which is possible because the ownership of bitcoin is concentrated in a relatively few hands, called "whales". This manipulation will be dealt with in the next Chapter 7. Here we will focus on false marketing and distraction.

To obscure the reality of bitcoin, those who promote its use mislead the public with the familiar magician's technique of distraction. A magician very cleverly draws the audience's attention to something irrelevant that he is doing in order to divert their eyes from his hocus pocus. Managing audience attention is critical to magic acts. With a diversion, such as a sleight-of-hand or his mesmerizing patter, an observer's focus will be on the irrelevant while the specifics of the trick go unnoticed. Magic 101 teaches you how to create illusions, present one tangential reality while concealing the central one. The first is misdirection, focusing the audience's attention on an unimportant but catchy comment, gesture, or object so that nobody notices the crux of the matter that is happening right before their eyes. Bitcoin is a magic trick. Promoters of bitcoin use a long list of distractions and illusions which we discuss below.

6.1. The brand "Bitcoin" and visual illusions

Most of us are very suggestible and product promoters count on that. Bitcoin's very name is ingenious marketing of a brand. Through massive marketing on various webpages and other media, the brand "Bitcoin" and its symbol of a coin containing the "B" that overlaps a dollar sign (see Figure 6.1) are well-known in large parts of the global population in both the developed and developing world. The word "coin" suggests that bitcoin is something tangible and that it is money.

Ƀbitcoin

Figure 6.1. Bitcoin logo and symbol. Source: Public domain.

Furthermore, bitcoin marketing uses the image of the glittering gold coin with the embossed bitcoin logo (see Figure 6.2). The gold coin image reinforces an idea that bitcoin is something valuable that you can hold in your hand. After people have seen the gold coin image hundreds of times, they start believing that bitcoin is actually something valuable and is money in the same sense as the US dollar or a real store of value, like gold. Even the abbreviation of bitcoin, "BTC", suggests that bitcoin is "money" since all other currencies also have three letter abbreviations, including USD, CAD, and EUR.

Figure 6.2. All that glitters is not gold....

Figure 6.3. … but gold always glitters. Real gold-coin ("Gold-gulden") from Mainz, Germany (1397-1419).

The use of the term "mining" by the promoters is also a brilliant distraction. The term suggests to people that the "coin" has somehow been "earned" through hard work — similar to normal gold-mining extraction from the earth and its smelting. The term "mining" suggests that bitcoin is worth at least the sum total of value of the electricity used (and computers purchased) to "create" that coin. Exponentially more and more electricity is planned to be needed to reach the full 21 million bitcoin in the expected next approximately 100 years (although the final date is debated and the bitcoin system may be altered). Some promoters actually use the fact that exponentially more electricity will be needed to mine the final bitcoins in order to explain why the price of bitcoin will skyrocket. That is nonsense. The electricity used is a sunk cost. Nothing valuable has been created with the expenditure of the electricity needed to "mine" bitcoin. The electricity has been wasted. It has simply been used to secure prior transactions. An article on Investopedia entitled, "What Determines the Price of 1 Bitcoin?" published May 2021 states, "bitcoin prices are influenced by the following factors:…The cost of producing a bitcoin through the mining process… ."

Moreover, there are alternative ways of securing the bitcoin network other than mining. However, changing to a new method would require agreement of most of the current mining computing power, who all have a vested interest in continuing to create bitcoin for themselves using the current method (mining). And, at the beginning of bitcoin, it was miners' wish to sell their mined bitcoin that initiated the market for bitcoin. Miners, who control the rules of bitcoin, are not easily going to decide to change bitcoin away from mining and put themselves out of business. So, for better or worse, bitcoin mining will remain.

6.2. Anonymity distraction

Much of the attraction to bitcoin is its still generally-perceived "anonymity" which promoters still promote despite the facts and wide-spread evidence to the contrary.

The limited anonymity (second-party anonymity) of bitcoin provides non-criminals with some benefits because identity theft is impossible with bitcoin (no one can steal your credit card number), you are not bombarded with advertisements each time you make a purchase giving your email address, and, when dealing with shady characters, anonymity keeps you protected from extortion and retaliation.

Bitcoin does not, however, have full third-party anonymity, particularly with respect to law enforcement. For example, as mentioned in section 4.5 above, the FBI was able to recover a significant part of the bitcoin ransom paid in the Colonial pipeline ransomware attack. Bitcoin's second-party anonymity has some benefits for criminals including tax evasion, terrorist financing, gun smuggling, human trafficking, and money laundering. However, governments can usually trace bitcoin transactions and learn the identity of the registered owner of an anonymous wallet through the use of their subpoena power. This applies to any bitcoin exchange in developed nations where customer identification laws apply. Further, in certain circumstances, private citizens are also able to obtain a court order requiring that bitcoin exchanges disclose customer information.

6.3. Blockchain and technobabble distraction

Whether we know it or not, human beings have the tendency to rely on the first piece of information that we received about something and staying with that, no matter how many times we hear the opposite. This is a form of cognitive bias that psychologists call 'anchoring'. Probably the first thing most of us hear about bitcoin is that it was a product of blockchain technology and, since blockchain is indeed a useful technology, bitcoin must be an excellent product. But marketing bitcoin as an offshoot of blockchain technology is another distraction. It is called attribute substitution, meaning that our attention is directed to one attribute of bitcoin (the blockchain) to the exclusion of all other attributes, such as that bitcoin has a bad function as money and is not an asset.

There is also the presentation of anecdotal material. Anecdotes are very convincing for most people. When someone tells you that their cousin made $1,000 in one day by investing in bitcoin, it is commonplace to believe that what happened to the guy's cousin could easily happen to you. This is called the base rate fallacy – the tendency to believe the outcome of one particular case and ignore the results of the majority of cases.

In bitcoin promotions, there is generally a lot of discussion about the blockchain technology behind bitcoin. However, the technology is irrelevant to usefulness. You can have very complex Rube Goldberg chain reaction contraptions that have no usefulness. What matters is a product's functionality not the sophistication that went into its manufacture. A car is a car regardless of whether it has an electric or combustion engine. Just as the smelting process of a gold coin is irrelevant to the question of whether the gold coin is real money, it is completely irrelevant to its value that bitcoin uses blockchain technology. Blockchain is just another distraction. Below, for example, are some typical quotations from a much larger technology section of a publication by Goldman Sachs called "Crypto: A new asset class?" The quotations, like most of the technology section, discuss blockchain technology – but are irrelevant to whether cryptocurrencies are a good investment for Goldman Sachs' clients.

"Beyond the software itself is the fact that the blockchains that underlie Bitcoin, Ethereum and other crypto networks have no central authority that controls them. Volunteers run nodes—entities that come to a distributed consensus—that accept transactions and attempt to get them incorporated into the blockchain. And then miners compete against each other to construct new blocks on the blockchain. The incentives in that distributed protocol are interesting and sensitive....

And even when secure code is deployed, if the functionality of the underlying blockchain has changed—which, for example, happens every few months on the Ethereum blockchain as it forks—that may inadvertently make existing contracts insecure. So a preponderance of evidence is needed to assess security. That means having an educated team with industry experience, security standards, authentication systems, key management, and regular external security reviews. A single data point isn't enough; security needs to be thought about holistically."

To their credit, the promoters do reveal a major technical problem with bitcoin, but, to their greater shame, irresponsibly wave away the possibility of the problem ever occurring. The problem is that, should the control of the majority of computing power in the bitcoin network, i.e., the mining activity, fall into the hands of a party that wished to destroy the network, the network would face total disruption and trust in bitcoin would quickly evaporate. Since bitcoin would lose trust, the market for and price of bitcoin would crash. This "impossible" situation can occur for a variety of reasons, most likely by a powerful government with a strategic geopolitical, national security and/or economic security motivation.

6.4. Distraction through various concepts

Bitcoin promoters call bitcoin the "new money" or "new store of value". As we explained in detail earlier, bitcoin is not money nor is it a store of value.

Another distraction is calling bitcoin an "investment". However, as bitcoin is not an asset, there is nothing to invest in. Since it is not an investment, no investment advisor credential or license is needed to promote the buying of bitcoin. Therefore, the bitcoin promotion market is left open to a vast number of self-interested bitcoin pumpers. Bitcoin promotion is similar to pyramid marketing. Once a person owns bitcoin, they are motivated to market bitcoin to their friends since greater demand for bitcoin will maintain or raise the price of what they themselves own.

Promoters further distract by criticizing "fiat money" – normal money like the US dollar – claiming that the government can "print an unlimited amount of it and nothing, now that it is off the gold standard, is backing it – but, in the case of bitcoin, there is a maximum limit of 21 million bitcoin." Fiat money does have limitations. However, as was concluded in Chapter 5, this does not give any support to buy bitcoin or other cryptocurrencies. Pointing out the limitations of fiat money is a diversion, a strategy of "look there" so that you do not see what is in front of you. It has been shown that the people most likely to be fooled by an illusionist's trick are those who are overconfident in their ability to "figure out" tricks. Their very confidence makes them blind.

Promoters contend that bitcoin can minimize transaction costs because it does away with the need for financial intermediaries. In fact, the intermediation of banks is just replaced by different intermediaries that charge different transactions fees, namely the bitcoin miners and exchanges (see Chapter 2). Except when making very large transactions, bitcoin transaction fees are higher than traditional banking system fees. The idea that there is supposed to be no middleman is an attractive one, but it happens not to be true.

Promoters have contended that bitcoin can be used for good purposes such as financing dissidents in foreign countries. In fact, dissidents and human rights advocates want untraceable real cash and those funding them know how to secretly get that cash to them. They do not want a permanent public ledger electronic trail that can be traced by a sophisticated repressive regime. Furthermore, dissidents generally do not have internet access or, at least not one that is uncensored and unmonitored. Thus, they cannot perform a swift and secure bitcoin transaction. Closer to home, we have never seen a single person or company "dissident" that has been cut off from the banking or credit-card systems who has then declared that they will now accept bitcoin.

Promoters also argue that bitcoin allows for "banking the unbanked." They argue that bitcoin provides access to markets to individuals in the developing world who are not well served by banks or central financial institutions. But most of the unbanked live in rural areas with no internet access. Furthermore, bitcoin transaction costs are too high for such small transactions. The unbanked are also likely to be poor and cannot risk the volatility of bitcoin prices. Individuals who fall for the rationalization that bitcoin can be of service to the poor or to persecuted dissidents suffer from compassion bias, which is the tendency to be especially touched by the plight of known or identifiable victims than by the unknown needs of an anonymous population.

Last, but not least, promotors claim that the bitcoin system is decentralized. Nothing could be more fake. In Chapter 7, we will show how small bitcoin owners are in the hands of, and handed over to, a group of whales who control the trade.

6.5. Summary

We regret that, to date, the promoters have been very successful with their false marketing and distraction tricks. The value of bitcoin has increased a massive amount during the last 10 years, despite that bitcoin has no function as money, is not an asset, and is not a hedge against anything.

The first trick is massive marketing of the brand "bitcoin", and its symbol of a coin containing the "B" that overlaps a dollar sign. The visual illusions of glittering coins and the sub-phrase "coin" give the impression that bitcoin is something valuable and tangible. We know it is not. Furthermore, the concept of "mining" attributes that one actually mines, by extracting, generating or otherwise creating, something valuable, such as gold, and that the costs of creating bitcoin justifies its value. This attribution is, as we show, nonsense.

Another trick is to direct attention to one attribute of bitcoin, for example, how it is created through blockchain technology, and exclude more fundamental attributes such as which function bitcoin has or does not have. Other distractions and false claims include "lowering transaction costs by doing away with the intermediaries", "anonymity", "financing dissidents in developing countries", and "banking the unbanked". None of these claims are true.

In summary, bitcoin is a magic trick where a massive number of promoters are deceiving gullible buyers with an illusionist's tricks. Unfortunately, the only real magic is a magician making your money disappear.

Bob Seeman and Roger Svensson

Chapter 7

Manipulation

s readers have already seen, the bitcoin industry uses a jargon of its own.

7.1. Strong concentration of owners

Large holders of bitcoin stock are called "whales" and they control most of the bitcoin wealth. In that sense, the "decentralization" of bitcoin is a promotional myth. Approximately 2% of bitcoin accounts control 95% of bitcoin. Of this 95%, cryptocurrency exchanges control about 7% of the bitcoin, with whales owning the balance, 88%.

Whales, so named due to the size of their bitcoin holdings, exert an outsized impact on the bitcoin market. One big trade by a whale (proportionally big, but small in their own eyes relative to the size of their bitcoin holdings) can significantly move the bitcoin price up or down – like real whales, they can make big splashes (see Picture 7.1). As a consequence, small investors are vulnerable to large price variations. It is in the interest of whales, of course, to liquidate very gradually, rather than flooding the market all at once, since a rapid liquidation would crash the price of bitcoin. However, they may decide to make huge waves if they needed the money quickly or they got spooked by a sudden change in the price of bitcoin, new regulation of the bitcoin network, a general stock market panic, or a geopolitical or other crisis.

Picture 7.1. Killer whales or orcas are actually members of the dolphin family and there are no documented cases of fatal attacks in the wild on humans. Photographer: Robert Pittman.

As long as financial markets have existed, there have always been people who have tried to manipulate them to their own advantage; bitcoin markets are no exception. Manipulation is easier to do with bitcoin because there are so few regulations and no direct oversight body, making the markets easy to fraudulently manipulate, making money laundering simpler and facilitating criminal activity. While interest in bitcoin trading grows, the threat of market abuse keeps many people understandably wary.

There are three forms of potential manipulation that need watching: wash trading/churning, "spoofing" and "pump and dump".

7.2. Wash trading

Wash trading/churning occurs when a trader buys and sells items that feed the market with misleading information, which leads to inaccurate reporting of trade volumes. This manipulation is done deliberately to make it falsely look as if large volumes were being traded. This is done to attract additional traders. In a March 2019 presentation to the U.S. Securities and Exchange Commission (SEC), Bitwise Asset Management claimed that the widely-used CoinMarketCap data were wrong, and that 95% of the reported volume consisted of non-economic trading or had been otherwise falsified.

Prosecutions for wash trading in cryptocurrencies have already taken place. In July 2020, the CEO, President, and Chief Operating Officer of Canadian cryptocurrency exchange, Coinsquare, were all forced to step down after the Ontario securities regulators accused the company of inflating trading by $5.5 billion. Coinsquare admitted that it had engaged in market manipulation by reporting inflated trading volumes. Between July 17, 2018, and December 4, 2019, Coinsquare reported approximately 840,000 wash trades, amounting to an estimated 590,000 bitcoins and representing over 90% of the reported trading volume on its platform. These trades were without economic basis, created for the sole purpose of inflating their reported trading volumes.

7.3. Spoofing

Spoofing is another form of market manipulation. Traders spoof or con market participants by entering orders with no intention to conduct real trades but, rather, to alter other people's trading behavior. You can spot spoofing when an unusually high amount of orders are entered over the course of a day and then deleted unexecuted by the end of the day.

Layering is when traders enter orders to buy and sell bitcoin at varying amounts and at different prices. These orders confuse market participants as to actual supply or demand. The layering traders wait for a market reaction, effect an order that takes advantage of the market reaction and immediately cancel the other orders. It has been reported that the U.S. Justice Department is currently working with the U.S. Commodity Futures Trading Commission (CFTC) regarding trades that manipulate the price of bitcoin and other cryptocurrencies using spoofing and layering methods.

7.4. Pump and dump

A third method is pump and dump. This method occurs when a person buys bitcoin and encourages others to also buy by disseminating misleadingly positive information about the asset, inciting more people to buy and, thus, boosting the price. Once the price rises to a sufficiently high level, the person sells. A report by the Wall Street Journal on August 5, 2018, stated that all cryptocurrency pump and dump schemes, taken together, accounted for $825 million in trading activity from January to July 2018, with hundreds of millions of dollars in subsequent losses to individuals. During the six-month period, there were 125 pump and dump operations, manipulating prices of 121 different cryptocurrencies. Traders involved in such pump and dump schemes form groups to instruct each other how to more effectively do this. The groups can be found on platforms such as Telegram and Discord. The Wall Street Journal article quoted Ben Yates, a cryptocurrency lawyer, stating that "Cryptocurrency exchanges are unregulated markets, so the kind of market manipulation banned on, say, the New York Stock Exchange, can essentially be carried out with impunity."

Furthermore, bitcoin exchanges themselves might sell from their own accounts against the interests of their customers, putting customers at a significantly unfair disadvantage.

7.5. Manipulation undermines trust

Manipulation undermines trust in financial markets. Trading is based on the fundamental principle that no participant has an unfair advantage over another. If participants' trust is undermined, they will not enter the market or will exit when they discover fraud – causing stakeholders to suffer major financial losses. The responsibility is on cryptocurrency exchanges to implement rigorous surveillance programs to identify and eliminate deceitful market behavior.

The CFTC Customer Advisory: Understand the Risks of Virtual Currency Trading as of May 18, 2021, in

Appendix D states that, "Virtual currency... value is completely derived by market forces of supply and demand, and they are more volatile than traditional fiat currencies." Fiat money, as discussed earlier, is normal government-issued money that is not backed by a physical commodity, such as gold, but rather by the backing of the issuing government. The CFTC advisory explains why buying bitcoin is riskier than fiat money: the buying and selling of bitcoin is not regulated or supervised by a government agency; the exchanges may lack sufficient critical system safeguards, including customer protection, the bitcoin price is volatile, with sharp falls occurring within extremely short time periods; and, in a flash crash, massive losses and recoveries can occur in a matter of minutes and even seconds. See also the March 26, 2021 CFTC press release in Appendix E entitled "Federal Court Orders UK Man to Pay More Than $571 Million for Operating Fraudulent Bitcoin Trading Scheme."

On January 14, 2021, Bloomberg published an article that academic research suggests bitcoin is influenced by fraudulent trading in a stablecoin called tether. A "stablecoin" is a cryptocurrency supposed to always have the same real U.S. dollar value. A 2019 report by finance professors John Griffin at University of Texas at Austin and Amin Shams of Ohio State University showed patterns between bitcoin's price and issuance of tether. The professors theorized that one large trader prints unbacked tether coins that are then traded for bitcoin, which increases the demand for and price of bitcoin. Tether has rejected the claims. The General Counsel of Tether has stated that, "Reports of manipulation of crypto markets by Tether are predicated on a paper that has been roundly discredited, ... Multiple other researchers have found, using superior methodologies, that there is no causal relationship between the issuance of Tethers and market movements up or down." The General Counsel of Tether stated that tether is always backed by traditional currency and cash, and that the increase in the price of bitcoin is being driven by increased buying by institutional investors. In April 2020, authors Richard

Lyons at the University of California, Berkeley and Ganesh Viswanath Natraj at the University of Warwick wrote in relation to tether that, "Issuance behavior can be explained as maintaining a decentralized system of exchange rate pegs and acting as a safe haven in the digital asset economy."

On February 23, 2021, New York Attorney General Letitia James entered into a settlement agreement with bitcoin exchange, Bitfinex, and Tether to end all trading activity with New Yorkers. The Attorney General stated that Tether represented that each of its Tether stablecoins were backed one-to-one by U.S. dollars in reserve. However, an investigation by the Office of the Attorney General found that Bitfinex and Tether made false statements about the backing of the tether stablecoin, and about the movement of hundreds of millions of dollars between the two companies to cover up massive losses by Bitfinex. The settlement agreement also required the companies to pay $18.5 million in penalties, in addition to requiring a number of steps to increase transparency.

Attorney General James said that "Bitfinex and Tether recklessly and unlawfully covered-up massive financial losses to keep their scheme going and protect their bottom lines. ... Tether's claims that its virtual currency was fully backed by U.S. dollars at all times was a lie."

There are also cybersecurity and security risks within the operation of the exchanges themselves. Several exchanges have lost hundreds of millions of dollars of bitcoin to cyber attackers or insider theft, threatening the security of each customer's account.

7.6. Summary

In summary, cash markets, such as the market for buying and selling bitcoin, are easy to manipulate. There are two main reasons: First, manipulation is easier to undertake with bitcoin than other financial markets because the bitcoin markets and exchanges are neither regulated nor supervised by any government agency. Second, the ownership of bitcoin is highly concentrated, where a few owners – called "whales" – control 88% of all the bitcoin. The behavior of the whales has a large impact on prices and trade. Thus, the decentralization of bitcoin is a promotional myth.

A variety of techniques exist for price manipulation: wash trading/churning means that traders buy and sell items that feed the market with misleading information, overestimating the trade volumes; spoofing implies entering fake orders to alter other people's trading behavior; and, pump and dump occurs when somebody buys an asset and thereafter disseminates false information about it to encourage others to buy it – and when the price increases sufficiently high, the initiator of the false information sells.

Cases of manipulation have already resulted in securities commission penalties and settlement agreements with government.

Bob Seeman and Roger Svensson

Chapter 8

Regulation

T rading and holding bitcoin both involve significant legal and regulatory risk for several reasons.

8.1. Crimes, money laundering and theft

To begin, bitcoin has been, and continues to be, used for illicit purposes such as buying and selling illegal, often lethal, drugs on the dark web, the "underground" internet.

> The dark web is a part of the internet that is accessed through the special, but easily available, Tor internet browser. Tor has, in part, been funded by the U.S. government since, for example, it enables research and communication by dissidents in foreign countries. While Tor itself is not illegal, a person might be more suspected of illegal activity if found to be using it. It is used by criminals because it helps prevent anyone knowing what websites you visit consisting as it does of more than seven thousand relays. A user's location and usage are, thus, largely protected from prying eyes.

Bitcoin is also used on the dark web by drug cartels for purposes of laundering profits. Rogue states such as Russia, Iran, and North Korea use bitcoin to fund cyberattacks, or avoid American and international sanctions, or simply to decrease governments in the West from exerting too much influence in the global marketplace. Bitcoin can provide terrorist organizations with a tool to circumvent traditional financial institutions in order to advance their nefarious missions by obtaining, transferring, and using funds to pay accomplices. Some terrorist groups have solicited millions of dollars of bitcoin donations through social media campaigns.

See Appendix A regarding the Department of Justice Cryptocurrency Enforcement Framework. Further, in the United States, the Commodity Futures Trading Commission (CFTC) has statutory authority with respect to certain aspects and uses of bitcoin. Under the Commodity Exchange Act (CEA), the CFTC has oversight over derivatives contracts, including futures, options, and swaps that involve a commodity and the CFTC has concluded that bitcoin is a commodity. The CFTC regulates manipulation of bitcoin marketplaces.

Many crimes that involve the use of bitcoin, such as buying and selling illicit drugs, are not new crimes but have been around for a very long time. The new part is that criminals are increasingly using bitcoin for these transactions. The illicit use of bitcoin can fall into three broad categories:

- Engaging in financial transactions associated with the commission of crimes, such as buying and selling drugs or weapons on the dark web, leasing servers for the purpose of committing cybercrimes, or soliciting funds to support terrorist activity;
- Engaging in money laundering or shielding otherwise legitimate activities from reporting requirements for tax or other reasons; and,
- Committing crimes, such as theft and manipulation, directly implicating the bitcoin marketplace itself.

Fraudsters also use bitcoin to swindle people similar to how fraudsters have swindled people throughout the ages. Similar scams use fiat money or other value such as store gift cards. While the existence of bitcoin often makes the swindles easier to conduct, since such scams are not unique to bitcoin, there is no need to discuss them in this book.

8.2. Crimes are hidden behind bitcoin transactions

Criminals use bitcoin to facilitate crimes and to avoid detection in ways that would be more difficult with fiat currency or "real money." They can avoid large, difficult-to-transport cash transactions and mitigate the risk of bank accounts being traced, or of banks notifying governments of suspicious activity. Criminals have used bitcoin, often in large amounts, and transferred it across international borders, as a new means to fund criminal behavior, which can range from human trafficking to fundraising for terrorist causes. Bitcoin is also used to pay for illegal drugs, firearms, and tools to commit cybercrimes, as well as to conduct sophisticated ransomware and blackmail crimes.

Cyberattackers using bitcoin can receive ransom and blackmail payments without large amounts of cash being transferred and potentially traced. Criminals routinely infect victims' computers and servers with ransomware, which is a type of malicious software designed to encrypt or otherwise block access to valuable data, only allowing access to data after the victim provides a specified payment (generally in bitcoin). Criminals demand similar types of payment by threatening to distribute confidential or purported embarrassing data (such as purported incriminating photos in cases of "sextortion") or engaging in "virtual kidnappings" where victims are misled into believing that a family member has been taken hostage.

On May 8, 2021, we all heard on the news that the Colonial Pipeline Company had halted its operations because of a ransomware attack. This interruption in the flow of gasoline disrupted critical gasoline supplies throughout the U.S. East Coast. Recently, ransomware attacks have been coupled with data breaches in which perpetrators also steal data from their targets. In addition to locking their computer systems, cyberattackers notify the victims that they have copies of their data and will release sensitive information unless a ransom is paid – thereby committing double extortion. Therefore, after paying up to unlock your data, you may be surprised with a second ransom demand not to release your data to the world. Colonial Pipeline was a victim of the DarkSide ransomware-as-a-service ("RaaS"). RaaS is a cybercrime model in which one criminal group develops the ransomware malware and hosts the computers from which it attacks other computers and leases that capability to another criminal group, who then conduct their attack.

If a person is charged with a crime, the government can seize, and forfeit bitcoin and other property derived from their illegal activity. See Appendix H for an example of an auction of seized bitcoin by the U.S. Marshal. U.S. statutory authorities for forfeiture include:

- Criminal forfeiture, 18 U.S.C. § 982; 21 U.S.C. § 853.
- Civil forfeiture, 18 U.S.C. § 981.

8.3. Money laundering and bitcoin laundering

Criminals are increasingly using bitcoin to launder their illicit proceeds. Money laundering occurs when an individual knowingly conducts a financial transaction linked to a crime in order to conceal the deal and its illegal gains or to evade federal reporting requirements. Illegal conduct can go under the radar when the transfer of funds takes place online with some anonymity. It is often easier to hide the transfer of funds with bitcoin than with fiat currency. The many online marketplaces that use bitcoin have provided criminals and terrorists with new opportunities to transfer their ill-gotten gains leaving less of a financial footprint. They can often get away with illicit doings much more easily now than ever before. Transnational criminal organizations, including drug cartels, find bitcoin especially attractive. Many criminals now move vast sums of money across international borders with little fear of detection. See Appendix F for the U.S. Department of the Treasury Financial Crimes Enforcement Network rule aimed at closing anti-money laundering regulatory gaps for specific forms of convertible virtual currency and digital assets. See also Appendix I.

Picture 8.1. Cash money confiscated due to money laundering.

Cash payments have more anonymity than bitcoin but have the difficulty of physically transporting large amounts of cash from one location to another, especially across national borders where baggage is examined.

Bitcoin gains from illegal activity have, themselves, to be laundered before they can be converted to money. If bitcoin is stolen from an exchange, received as ransom or acquired through other illegal activity, a criminal needs to launder it in order to convert it to real money that can be legitimately spent. The purpose of money laundering services is to obscure the identities of both seller and buyer.

Bitcoin can be laundered using "mixers, "scramblers," "tumblers" or other similar techniques such as "chain hopping." Such activities are done by software or services that are able to mix the coins of one user with those of another and thereby obscure the connection between bitcoin transactions, bitcoin addresses and personal identity so that privacy and secrecy is enhanced. A common technique, the "mixer," refers to taking in bitcoin from multiple customers and mixing them together in a figurative "pot". The mixer operator typically takes a small percentage of the proceeds as a transaction fee and returns the balance in a series of random transactions in an approximately pro-rata fashion with a view to severing the traceability between the bitcoin thrown in the pot and the bitcoin thrown back. Mixing can be spotted and overcome by sophisticated law enforcement technology and personnel. Any mixed bitcoin can, therefore, become suspect such that legitimate financial institutions may not want to accept it. For investigation purposes, law enforcement may even take over operation of a mixer that they identify, a huge risk to money launderers.

Gambling sites that accept bitcoin are also used to launder bitcoin. A criminal may establish an account and then transfer funds to the gambling site. He will then make simple bets at the site before withdrawing his funds to a new bitcoin address. This process creates a break in the bitcoin flow, making it harder to trace the chain back to the original owner. However, if the gambling site route (or other money laundering route) is spotted in the history of transactions (remember that everything is publicly recorded on the bitcoin blockchain), this raises a red flag for law enforcement.

In the United States, relevant laws include:

- Money laundering, 18 U.S.C. § 1956 et seq.
- Transactions involving proceeds of illegal activity, 18 U.S.C. § 1957.
- Operation of an unlicensed money transmitting business, 18 U.S.C. § 1960.
- Failure to comply with Bank Secrecy Act requirements, 31 U.S.C. § 5331 et seq.

8.4. Tax evasion

Bitcoin transactions can also facilitate tax evasion. Tax cheats may think that the Internal Revenue Service is not able to uncover or know to whom to attribute their bitcoin gains. They may attempt tax evasion by, among other things, failing to report capital gains from the sale of their bitcoin, not reporting business income received in bitcoin, not reporting wages paid in bitcoin, or using bitcoin to facilitate false invoice schemes designed to fraudulently reduce business income. Tax loss from such unreported capital gains become increasingly significant as new cryptocurrencies emerge, especially since their market price constantly fluctuates.

On May 21, 2021, the Treasury issued a report calling for bitcoin transfers worth more than $10,000 to be reported to the Internal Revenue Service (IRS). The report stated, "Although cryptocurrency is a small share of current business transactions, such comprehensive reporting is necessary to minimize the incentives and opportunity to shift income out of the new information reporting regime."

8.5. Terrorist financing and avoiding economic sanctions

Bitcoin transactions may also be prosecuted if they are used as a means of providing material support to terrorists or foreign terrorist organizations. Such transactions could also be used for payments that facilitate crimes that pose a danger to national security, such as espionage or conspiracies involving interference in the political process.

Individuals, companies, and states may use bitcoin in an attempt to avoid the reach of U.S. economic sanctions. Bitcoin's peer-to-peer format may allow individuals to bypass the financial controls that enforce rule of law sanctions and that are built into the international banking system. Several states have explored the creation and use of their own state-sponsored cryptocurrencies, which could serve as further platforms that evade financial controls. Venezuela attempted to launch a national cryptocurrency similar to bitcoin – called the "Petromoneda" or "Petro" – in the hope that it would allow Venezuela to circumvent U.S. sanctions. Other countries may do the same.

8.6. Bitcoin theft

The lack of transparency in the bitcoin market makes it particularly attractive for thieves. Criminals and rogue state actors can steal bitcoin by exploiting security vulnerabilities in wallets and exchanges. Cyberattackers can attack wallets and exchanges directly, using social engineering (fooling people) and a variety of other methods to obtain passwords and PINs. If the criminals operate exchanges, they can themselves engage in insider theft. This susceptibility to theft on a massive scale should make people wary. It demonstrates that the lack of appropriate regulation and monitoring of bitcoin exchanges poses a threat to bitcoin users themselves, as well as to the general public.

John Booth, a lawyer, financier and fintech CEO based in London, argues that there may be a significant chain of title legal issue with stolen bitcoin. In most common law jurisdictions, if someone steals your watch and then that watch is sold many times over to only honest innocent people, the watch is still your watch. It is stolen goods belonging to you. The final honest buyer, when the watch is identified by you, is out of luck. You can demand your watch back from the person holding it and go to court to enforce that demand. However, in contrast, imagine if someone steals your *money* and that money is used multiple times between only honest innocent people. The result will vary based on the precise situation and jurisdiction, but the honest holder of the money who provided good value, such as a product, in return for the money will likely never have to pay that money back to you. Governments have an interest in setting the rules so that their fiat currency is able to be widely honored as final payment to honest people providing value. The difference in outcomes is because a watch is a watch and money is money. Bitcoin is not money. Bitcoin is a record of transactions. Bitcoin is, therefore, more like an item like watch. Therefore, unless, before any bitcoin transaction, you first carefully check the complete history of the bitcoin that you are considering accepting, that bitcoin may essentially be the proceeds of crime and is subject to repossession by the true owner from whom it was stolen. The bitcoin public ledger makes tracing all bitcoin transactions easier than tracing cash.

8.7. Cryptojacking

Cybercriminals will even attack and hijack company computers or individual computers and use them to mine their bitcoin. That means that a computer's processing and electrical power is harnessed and stolen by the cyberattacker. Cryptojacking malware is software that infects computers in order to use them to mine bitcoin, usually without a user's knowledge. Computers hijacked in this way will operate slower and can crash due to the extra strain on computational resources.

Since bitcoin is often the preferred payment method for the distribution of illegal goods and services, and for the collection of funds from victims of traditional fraud or computer intrusions, the United States may impose a wide variety of federal charges on such activities including:

- Wire fraud, 18 U.S.C. § 1343.
- Mail fraud, 18 U.S.C. § 1341.
- Securities fraud, 15 U.S.C. §§ 78j and 78ff.
- Access device fraud, 18 U.S.C. § 1029.
- Identity theft and fraud, 18 U.S.C. § 1028.
- Fraud and intrusions in connection with computers, 18 U.S.C. § 1030.

8.8. China's bitcoin bans

In June 2021, China banned bitcoin mining. China's biggest concern about mining was the use of bitcoin as a way of avoiding China's strict currency export restrictions of 50,000 USD per person per year. A bitcoin miner in China who was able to access a large amount of cheap electricity could mine bitcoin and then sell the bitcoin on exchanges outside the country. Therefore, the miner would obtain money that is outside China and thereby avoiding China's currency export restrictions. The miner, thus, converts money in China into electricity in China, into bitcoin, and then into money outside China. This avoidance of the currency export restrictions limits the government's ability to control the value of their currency and the effect of their laws.

Previously, on May 18, 2021, the National Internet Finance Association of China, the China Banking Association and the Payment and Clearing Association of China issued a joint statement that no institution, including banks and online payments channels, could offer clients any service involving bitcoin. Forbidden services include registration, trading, clearing and settlement. Banks are not to provide saving, trust or pledging services nor issue financial products related to bitcoin.

The statement read, "Recently, cryptocurrency prices have skyrocketed and plummeted, and speculative trading of cryptocurrency has rebounded, seriously infringing on the safety of people's property and disrupting the normal economic and financial order." The statement highlighted the risks of cryptocurrency trading, warning that bitcoin is "not supported by real value," that prices are easily manipulated, and that Chinese law does not protect the trading.

In June 2021, the government quickly started making moves against people who traded illegally in cryptocurrencies, including arresting 1,100 people.

China has not banned ownership or transfer of cryptocurrencies yet. Individuals can still hold bitcoin and trade it outside China.

8.9. Significant legal and regulatory risk

On May 7, 2021, Gary Gensler, the new chairman of the Securities and Exchange Commission (SEC), stated that he believed that more bitcoin regulation is required in order to prevent fraud and related issues. Bitcoin, he said, is "a digital, scarce store of value, but highly volatile... and there's investors that want to trade that, and trade that for its volatility, in some cases just because it is lower correlation with other markets. I think that we need greater investor protection there." Gensler said that he believes bitcoin is a "speculative" store of value and there should be a regulator to oversee exchanges, similar to the equity and futures markets. He said many cryptocurrencies were trading as if they were assets and should fall under the purview of the SEC.

On May 25, 2021, Federal Reserve Vice Chair of supervision Randal Quarles told the Senate Banking Committee that the Federal Reserve is in a "high priority" "sprint" alongside other US financial regulators to tighten supervision of cryptocurrencies like bitcoin. Federal Reserve Chairman Jerome Powell told the Committee that cryptocurrencies pose risks to the stability of the global financial system.

We must also keep in mind that China is a major economic and military power. China's bans may extend to other countries where China has influence and may also give ideas to other countries where it does not.

As a relatively new technology, there are, as yet, relatively few specific regulations designed with bitcoin in mind. At the same time, there are many current legal issues involving a variety of different U.S. agencies that affect the bitcoin marketplace. Regulations of various sorts apply, depending on the applicable country of the transaction. All such regulations are likely to change over time in different jurisdictions around the world. Trading bitcoin, thus, involves significant legal and regulatory risk.

8.10. Summary

Association with illegal activity is a major downside to the use of bitcoin in legitimate transactions and there is significant legal and regulatory risk in trading in bitcoin. Crimes are hidden behind bitcoin transactions. Money laundering and bitcoin laundering occur all the time. Tax evasion, terrorist financing, and avoiding economic sanctions are facilitated by bitcoin. Bitcoin is stolen and cryptojacking steals computing power and electricity to mine bitcoin. Since June 2021, there have been severe regulatory crackdowns in China. New regulations around the world, including the United States, will only increase. Such regulations may be so severe as to cripple the bitcoin network.

Chapter 9

It's just gambling

B itcoin is not money, not a store of value, and not an asset. What, then, is it? People are spending money to buy bitcoin and either making or losing money when they sell it. As this business model of money resembles gambling, it is worth asking, "Is this gambling?"

9.1. Gambling criteria

Each jurisdiction has a different definition of gambling. In general, gambling is engagement in an activity that meets the following criteria:

- A game of chance as distinguished from a game of skill.
- A person must pay money in exchange for a chance of financial gain.
- Money must change hands.
- More than a handful of people need to be involved.

9.2. Gambling vs. skill

Playing blackjack at a major casino is gambling since it is almost all based on the luck of the draw. Experience makes you slightly better at making the most of the hand you draw, but the game remains far more chance than skill.

Picture 9.1. Blackjack gambling

Playing poker is a gambling game even though there is a substantial element of skill involved in the betting strategy and in being able to read the give-away expressions on people's faces. That is where the expression "poker face" comes from. The more poker-faced you are, the greater your luck, but it is still a game of luck that depends on the hand that you are dealt.

Lotteries, roulette, craps, and slot machines are pure luck as they rely entirely on the spin of a wheel, the roll of a dice, or other computerized or physical method of generating a random outcome.

Betting on horse racing also is generally considered to be a specific type of gambling. While effort and expertise are involved in studying the past histories of horses and jockeys to arrive at winning probabilities, the betting system, often regulated, adjusts the odds to make the betting fairer amongst all betters. For similar reasons, betting on the outcome of any sporting match is generally considered to be gambling.

Trading company stocks, bonds, or commodities such as gold on the stock market is not gambling since there is a wealth of evidence that skilled traders, often employed full-time by the large Wall Street investment banks and paid handsomely, predict stock market rallies and declines much more accurately than the average stock trader. These professional traders generally rely on an extensive amount of detailed analysis of investment options, including the financial performance and public disclosures of the companies that they invest in and the projected demand for specific commodities by industry.

Currency trading is not gambling since professional currency traders analyse the economies, economic policies, trade, and politics of various countries and how these affect the value of their currency. Again, the professional traders at the big investment banks perform better than an average trader since they are more skilled at analyzing the information.

A Monopoly® game with real money, but between friends, is generally not considered to be gambling by the government. However, if a casino opened such a game to the public, it would be gambling. Betting on the outcome of a coin toss among friends is generally not gambling since, again, it is among friends and the number of people involved are few.

Store promotional contests where winners are randomly selected are designed to avoid gambling laws. To avoid such laws, the contests often do not require a purchase (i.e. spending any money). The contest also often adds a "skill testing question" in an attempt to make it something other than a game of chance. If you have learned nothing else from this book, you have just learned why silly "skill testing questions" are added to such contests.

9.3. Classic bubble

Bitcoin resembles a classic bubble. First, there is always a price explosion. The South Sea Company stock, for instance, soared 10-fold in 1720 due to rumors about extraordinary potential trade in the New World (America) and the share speculation that ensued.

All great bubbles seem to take place during periods when money is readily flowing, when interest rates are either very low or falling, and when people have a lot of liquid cash in their possession. This situation has never been truer than at present when central banks have had negative interest rates and flooded the market with money through bond purchases. In 17th century Holland, these conditions also prevailed and the price of tulips rose to unbelievable heights before quickly collapsing. This phenomenon was called tulipmania and is still the accepted term for economic bubbles built on assets of little value. A specially bred and rarely colored tulip bulb is at least an asset of some value since it can be grown and multiplied. Bitcoin cannot.

Speculation goes wild when an asset is impossible to properly value. Bitcoin, which has no cash flow or utility, cannot be assigned a fundamental value (see Chapter 5). Furthermore, it has a restricted supply (see Chapter 5), and the ownership is concentrated in relatively few hands (see Chapter 7). Thus, bitcoin is a speculator's dream.

When the price goes up too high, it is always due for a fall. During tulipmania, when the tulip boom ended, the price of bulbs fell by 99.8 percent. Given that bitcoin has less intrinsic value than a tulip bulb, a decline of similar magnitude is predictable.

9.4. The random walk of bitcoin – a game of chance

Absent illegal market manipulations, the price of bitcoin price varies randomly depending entirely on capricious fluctuations of supply and demand. The game is to guess when those ups and downs will occur. Analyzing a company's profit trajectory, the general state of the economy, or industry demand for a commodity to determine the value of assets is not available to the bitcoin trader because bitcoin has neither any underlying cash flow nor utility. Thus, bitcoin, to the average trader who is not in some way manipulating the market, is a game of pure chance. Bitcoin traders make pure guesses. Will others want to buy or sell? Do others think the bitcoin price will go up or down? The guesswork is in predicting the actions of a large number of humans who, in their turn, are all doing the same thing – guessing public sentiment on a particular day and time.

Sports gambling, such as on professional football, is a great analogy to the gambling occurring with bitcoin. Given that the point spread between the winning team and losing team that a person bets on changes automatically based on others' bets, similar to bitcoin, people are betting on how *others* think the football game will end.

There is no skill involved with bitcoin trading. It is more like flipping a coin. Only illegal manipulation of the market will give someone an edge on a bitcoin trade (see Chapter 7).

While, in 2011, when we first learned of bitcoin, we thought that it might be a Ponzi scheme, it is technically not a Ponzi – since it is open public knowledge that there are no assets or entity behind bitcoin that would, or could, pay back bitcoin purchasers. Nassim Taleb, the author of "The Black Swan", therefore, has coined a term for bitcoin – an "Open Ponzi".

9.5. Bitcoin is unlicensed gambling

There is no evidence that anyone, due to their skill, has made more money from bitcoin than less skilled people. Bitcoin is gambling since it meets all the gambling criteria: a game of chance where people use money to buy bitcoin, financial gain is sought, money changes hands, and many people participate.

Most people buy and sell bitcoin through exchanges which facilitate the transfer of bitcoin from the seller's bitcoin wallet to the buyer's in return for a transaction fee. One bitcoin exchange has made a public disclosure that its platform may be exploited to facilitate illegal activity such as fraud, money laundering, gambling, tax evasion, and scams. The disclosure states that the exchange may be subject to governmental inquiries, enforcement actions, prosecuted, or otherwise held secondarily liable for aiding or facilitating such activities. This disclosure is probably intended to cover the use of bitcoin by individuals who buy bitcoin on the exchange and engage in illegal gambling elsewhere. However, the disclosure may also serve to some extent to try to protect the exchange itself in the event that a government regulatory body investigates whether the bitcoin network itself, including bitcoin exchanges, is a form of gambling, legal or otherwise.

Any individual or organisation that is operating the bitcoin ecosystem and takes a transaction fee, including miners, bitcoin exchanges, bitcoin funds, and investment banks might be investigated for operating an illegal gambling enterprise. The legal argument would be that these entities – by taking a cut of the transaction – are acting as "The House", i.e., the casino, and are actually operating an unlicensed gambling enterprise and must obtain any license required in every jurisdiction in the world that they operate. Otherwise, all such miners, bitcoin exchanges, bitcoin funds, and investment banks must shutter operations in each jurisdiction where they have no required license.

9.6. Regulation and taxation of bitcoin as unlicensed gambling

Jurisdictions generally ban all gambling but, at the same time, permit certain specific types of gambling and require the gambling operators to obtain a license from the government which subjects them to regulation, oversight, and gambling-specific taxation. Licensed gambling is supervised by a specific government agency.

Gambling regulations generally require that the casino operate the games in specific ways to make sure that the players are treated fairly. The regulations, for example, require that rules of gambling games be fair, clearly specified, and publicly disclosed. All players must have the same chance to win and be able, in advance, to calculate their chances of winning.

In the State of Nevada, licensed gambling operators are subject to a special tax on monthly gross gambling revenues.

Licensed, regulated, and taxed gambling operators, such as licensed casinos in Las Vegas, may not be happy with the competition from the huge global bitcoin unlicensed gambling ecosystem which does not comply with gambling regulations and avoids required gambling-specific taxes. In the State of Nevada where Las Vegas is located, licensed gambling establishments must pay a special additional tax based on their monthly *gross* revenues.

The gambling industry in the United States is a very powerful industry group and has the ear of state governments and the federal government.

The determination of what is gambling will vary by jurisdiction. In some countries or states in the world, bitcoin could easily be found, in the future if not soon, to constitute illegal gambling.

In the United States, if bitcoin is found to be the proceeds of illegal gambling and a crime, and the bitcoin is transferred between states, it is possible that the federal laws on the inter-state transfer of proceeds of crime, which are in part set out in Chapter 8, may then apply.

The potential of a government in any jurisdiction in the world finding that the buying and selling of bitcoin is gambling is a supplementary legal and regulatory risk of bitcoin trading.

9.7. Summary

An activity is gambling if it meets all the following criteria: a game of chance where people use money to buy bitcoin, financial gain is sought, money changes hands, and many people participate. Casino games like blackjack, poker, roulette as well as lotteries and betting on horse races all meet these criteria.

Since bitcoin has no underlying cash flow or utility that can be analysed, its price movements are similar to a random walk. For the average bitcoin trader – who is not a whale with possibilities to illegally manipulate the market – trade is pure guessing or gambling. All the gambling criteria are met for bitcoin.

Many governments around the world regulate and levy special taxes respecting gambling such as a tax on monthly gross gambling revenues. No jurisdiction in the world has yet revealed if it has investigated any entity involved in operating the bitcoin ecosystem for compliance with gambling regulations. We determine that bitcoin trading is unlicensed and, thus, not specifically taxed gambling. New players redeem those who entered earlier. It is a zero-sum game. We are confident that, at some point, some jurisdictions will investigate entities operating the bitcoin ecosystem for compliance with their gambling regulations.

Bob Seeman and Roger Svensson

Chapter 10

Less than worthless

The bitcoin system wastes vast amounts of electricity. As miners compete to win the verification reward, massive amounts of computing power and electricity are lost. As was explained in Chapter 2, only one of a vast number of miners will verify each transaction and be rewarded with the transaction fee and newly minted bitcoin. However, all mining contenders will run their computers and consume electricity.

10.1. Electrical power wasted

So much computing power is needed by the bitcoin network for the mining that, as of July 1, 2021, its energy consumption exceeds that expended by Venezuela, 365 days a year and 24 hours a day. The Cambridge Centre for Alternative Finance estimates that bitcoin mining consumes about 65 terawatt-hours of energy annually. This unimaginably high amount of electricity is a concern for environmentalists especially since the energy used in this way produces nothing. It simply audits a single decentralized ledger, something that the centralized ledger system of the VISA® system, for instance, can do more efficiently, using tens of thousands of times less energy per transaction. VISA can verify the transaction in one second whereas it can take about ten minutes for a bitcoin transaction to be verified.

The wasted electricity used by the bitcoin network has an alternative use in other sectors, such as heating of houses and offices, industry production, transports, and air conditioning. By pushing up energy prices, the bitcoin network exerts negative externalities on other sectors.

Since the bitcoin network creates no value, the production of each bitcoin actually destroys value due to the vast electricity consumption. Thus, bitcoin has a *negative value* for the society as a whole.

As the University of Cambridge Centre for Alternative Finance ("CAF") states:

> "[I]n order to preserve [the] decentralised nature [of bitcoin], and as a result its censorship resistance, **Bitcoin precisely needs to be inefficient** in order prevent a single entity or colluding group of actors to easily gain control and dominate the network....
>
> Many electricity consumption estimates include comparisons with traditional payment systems. These may initially seem appropriate given that Bitcoin is often touted as global payment network. However, a closer look at the value proposition of these systems reveals substantial differences: unlike traditional payment systems, Bitcoin is designed to function as an open censorship-resistant value transfer system that anyone can access without requiring permission. **Achieving these properties requires engaging in different trade-offs which, as mentioned previously, necessarily results in massive operational costs and inefficiencies.**" [emphasis added]

When bitcoin prices are increasing, more miners are incentivized to participate in validating transactions and win the rights to publish the next block and collect the newly minted bitcoin and fees. This process has led to more miners and more investment in faster mining computers that use more energy. More miners and more energy required to power their computers has led to skyrocketing electricity needs. Such high energy consumption can lead to high negative externalities where purchasing electricity may not fully reflect all societal costs, including pollution from electricity production and any government subsides for power generation. There are often government subsidies for green energy. A kilowatt-hour of electricity generated by a coal-fired power station has substantially different carbon dioxide emissions (see Picture 10.1) than a kilowatt-hour made by solar cells. There are also other government subsidies for energy production to help create local employment. However, bitcoin mining produces extremely few permanent local jobs, usually just a handful of security guards and low-level computer technicians to replace burned out mining machines. Governments and taxpayers do not like their green energy and job-creation subsidies, paid in real money, being used for electricity that is being purposely wasted to create nothing of value, specifically something that is not money.

Figure 10.1. Coal burning power plant

Mining bitcoin is wasteful of electricity since bitcoin uses "proof-of-work" ("PoW") mining. Miners who wish to make decisions regarding the network need to prove that they performed some "work". As discussed, the work is finding the solution to a cryptographic puzzle which is essentially guessing a random number, and the only way to determine the correct random number is to try all options. The more miners in the game, the more difficult the puzzle becomes. Miners operate specialized mining computers that have been specifically designed to be very good at the single task of solving the PoW puzzle. The entrepreneur from 2011 in Chapter 1 had designed one of the first such specialized mining computers.

The main cost of PoW mining is the electricity to run mining computers. The more computers that a miner operates, the more likely she is to find the solution to the puzzle. However, more computers mean that more electricity is needed to operate the computers, which results in higher costs. Miners always seek the most inexpensive electricity sources. Miners also try to have the latest and most efficient machines to save on electricity. However, miners use different mining machines models that have different energy efficiencies. Mining also requires electricity to cool the computers to prevent them from overheating.

10.2. Towards cheaper and pollution-intensive energy sources

As time goes by and the bitcoin network approaches the 21 million ceiling, it will become more difficult to solve the mathematical puzzle necessary to verify bitcoin transactions. Even more electricity power will then be needed. Thus, mining will become more and more costly. Since miners try to minimize their electricity costs, they will locate their mining equipment in countries where energy is cheap and energy taxes are low (and the outside average temperature is cold so as to keep down electricity costs for cooling). Unsurprisingly, most mining until June 2021 occurred in regions and countries as western China and Ukraine, where energy costs are low. In China, taxes on coal-fired power-stations are low, and consequently, coal with high carbon dioxide emissions was the main source of energy for the bitcoin network. As discussed however, in June 2021 China banned bitcoin mining. If electricity costs become higher in a country or a government bans mining, miners will try to find other countries offering low energy costs or low taxes on electricity. There is an imminent risk that these will be countries that supply fossil fuels at low prices. The consequence would be high carbon dioxide emissions and pollution.

10.3. The waste of computers and chips

It is not only energy that is wasted when mining bitcoin. To be competitive, miners must purchase computer technology that is both energy-efficient and fast enough to solve the mathematical puzzle. The complexity of solving the puzzle continues to increase. As a result, it is not sufficient to mine bitcoin using a home computer as was possible in 2011, but one, instead, needs a whole wall of specialized mining computers to be competitive. The more and faster computers, the higher probability to solve the puzzle.

On June 19, 2021, The Economist's article "Pay to play" discussed the huge increase in prices and price volatility of graphics processing units (GPUs). Such GPUs are specialized chips that calculate matrix algebra, useful both for machine learning tasks as translating languages and 3D graphics. GPUs are also the best chips to use for mining the next most popular cryptocurrency, ethereum (but not bitcoin). Not all cryptocurrencies require mining but, like bitcoin, ethereum does. Statistics show that the price of used GPUs listed on Amazon, have risen from approximately 100 to 400 USD during the last two years. This price also correlates with the price of ethereum, both in ups and downs. The over-use of GPUs has caused a shortage in the market, creating bottlenecks, and impairs other sectors dependent of GPUs, such as data scientists, gamers, and computer-aided design users. Similarly, the demand for computer processing chips specialized to mine bitcoin – application specific integrated circuits (ASICs) – has also increased and impairs other sectors.

10.4. Summary

The bitcoin network wastes huge amounts of electricity. The main reasons are that the system has a decentralized and costly ledger to secure, and that all miners who compete to solve the mathematical puzzle must operate their mining computers and consume electricity. Today, the whole bitcoin system consumes in a year as much energy as Venezuela consumes in a year.

As the mathematical puzzle automatically and regularly becomes more complex, mining becomes more complex and more electricity is needed. Therefore, miners locate their equipment in countries with low energy costs and low taxes on fossil energy. The risk is that more electricity for mining will be sourced from fossil fuels with high carbon dioxide emissions. The electricity and computer equipment (chips) have alternative usage in other sectors. The vast mining creates large negative externalities on other sectors in terms of higher prices and shortages for both electricity and chips.

Since the bitcoin system does not produce any output that is useful for society but has vast negative externalities on other sectors, the societal value is negative. Bitcoin is less than worthless.

Bob Seeman and Roger Svensson

Chapter 11

Conclusions

Our main conclusion in this book is that bitcoin is nothing more and nothing less than gambling. The analysis shows that the functions as money, an asset, a store of value and a hedge against anything can completely be ruled out. Almost everything else one reads about bitcoin is either utopian fantasy, wishful thinking, nonsense, marketing, technobabble, or false propaganda.

11.1. Failure as money

Bitcoin does not represent any new money or payment system. The purpose of money is to reduce transaction costs for payments, loans, and relative valuations, which requires a stable value. These rules applied in 9,000 BCE just as they do today. The price is so extremely volatile that bitcoin is useless as a store of value, as a unit of account, and as a standard of deferred payments. Furthermore, transaction costs are too high, especially the time component, and set limitations for bitcoin as a medium of exchange. Thus, bitcoin increases, instead of reduces, transaction costs.

Because bitcoin is not issued by a central government, has a limited legal tender and a face value far above its intrinsic value, it is like token money. Unlike the historical token coins that had a function as small change and were convertible into a currency or a commodity, bitcoin lacks both these features. Bitcoin is useless even as token money. Finally, historical records show that a decentralized monetary system with tokens existed several hundred years ago, so even the claim of bitcoin as the first decentralized money system is false.

Furthermore, the claim that the bitcoin system has abandoned intermediaries is also false. Intermediaries exist. The miner who verifies the transaction charges a transaction fee and is an intermediary. The only difference is that the selection of the specific miner is essentially random, but the winning miner is an intermediary nevertheless. Close to 1% of bitcoin transactions are used for real-world purchases and there are more illegitimate purchases than legitimate. Any true utility of bitcoin for the tiny fraction of one percent of transactions representing legitimate purchases is far outweighed by the massive risk to the average individuals who speculate in this risky game.

11.2. Failure as an asset

Bitcoin is not an asset. Tangible and intangible assets have cash flow or utility that produce positive economic values. Based on the present value of the cash flow and utility, the fundamental value of the asset can be calculated. This applies to shares, real estate, bonds, and intellectual property. Bitcoin provides neither any cash flow nor utility. Thus, no fundamental value can be estimated for bitcoin. Bitcoin simply lacks an intrinsic value.

Bitcoin is not digital gold. An asset that is negatively correlated with real estate and shares would be ideal to include in a diversified portfolio. Historically, gold has had this role. It is regarded as among the safest investments in a crisis, is an excellent inflation hedge, and is the best-known store of value. The claim that bitcoin is "the digital gold" and will replace gold as a portfolio diversifier lacks any scientific evidence. Its pro-cyclical price movements rule out this. The high volatility and price drops of bitcoin of 50 % in both 2018 and 2021 are unmatched by any of the main fiat currencies in the last 50 years. Thus, bitcoin is no inflation-hedge. Therefore, our conclusion is that the large ups and downs in the bitcoin price depend on speculative gambling and rely on the greater fool theory.

Furthermore, the argument that scarcity creates value is nonsense. To create something that is rare in an artificial way is not difficult at all. Anyway, today, there are already 4,000 cryptocurrencies, and more coming all the time. Finally, there is no responsible issuer. So, if the bitcoin system breaks down, holders have nobody from whom to claim – or to whom to assign blame.

11.3. Distraction and manipulation

Although bitcoin has no function in society, the promoters have been very successful with false marketing and distraction tricks: the value of bitcoin has increased a massive amount during the last 10 years.

Massive marketing of the brand "bitcoin", its symbol of a coin containing the "B" that overlaps a dollar sign, the visual illusions of glittering coins and the sub-phrase "coin" give the impression that bitcoin is something valuable and tangible. Furthermore, the concept of "mining" attributes that one actually mines, by extracting, generating or otherwise creating, something valuable, such as gold, and that the costs of creating bitcoin justifies its value. Nothing of this is true.

Another trick is to direct attention to one attribute of bitcoin, for example, how it is created through blockchain technology (technobabble) and exclude more fundamental attributes such as which function bitcoin has or does not have.

Manipulation of the bitcoin market also damages the average bitcoin investor. This manipulation is possible since proper regulation and supervision are lacking, and the ownership of bitcoin is highly concentrated. Price manipulation techniques include wash trading/churning (providing misleading trade information), spoofing (entering fake orders), and pump and dump (buy, disseminate false information, sell). Several cases of manipulation have already resulted in securities commission penalties and settlement agreements with government.

11.4. Policy recommendation: Immediately investigate compliance with existing gambling regulations

The anonymity of bitcoin wallets facilitates using bitcoin for illegal activities. Crimes, money laundering, tax evasion, terrorist financing, and avoiding economic sanctions are hidden behind bitcoin transactions. Since June 2021, there have been severe regulatory crackdowns in China. New regulations around the world, including the United States, will only increase. Such regulations may be so severe as to cripple the bitcoin network. However, gambling is the major problem of bitcoin.

Credulous people are taking the bait and gambling away their life savings. Every day that this bubble is allowed to grow, many thousands more innocent bystanders are drawn into a game where only the House – those operating the bitcoin gambling casino – wins. Many people are winning in the bitcoin casino, especially the big traders and whales who can manipulate the market. However, no one is looking after the average punter.

Gambling is regulated in the United States and throughout much of the world. When will the gambling regulators step in to investigate bitcoin gambling? Time is of the essence. A bitcoin industry survey report in April 2021 stated that the "crypto-curious audience is ...63% of U.S. adults... [and] roughly 13% of U.S. adults plan to purchase cryptocurrency in the next 12 months." The industry has, thus, identified their next 12 month pool of "greater fools". A survey conducted by RIWI, a data analytics company, from May 24 to June 26, 2021, of 4,883 Americans showed that 16% consider bitcoin to be a great investment, 19% consider it to be "a scam", and the balance do not know.

Dangerously, an appreciable number of people are starting to consider bitcoin as part of their retirement investments. In May 2021, a popular investor information service for the retail investor suggested in an article, shockingly entitled "Is Bitcoin Safer for Retirement than

Social Security", that bitcoin, alongside traditional investments, and Social Security, might actually be a viable investment for retirement. Some investors are even borrowing to increase their bitcoin holdings or using their bitcoin as collateral for loans. Princeton University economist Markus Brunnermeier, stated on May 7, 2021, that when bitcoin becomes used as a retirement investment, "Many people would lose a whole lot of money, and they might question the whole system. Why didn't anybody protect them?"

It is time for gambling regulators in every jurisdiction in the world to investigate for compliance with their existing regulations every entity subject to their authority that operates the bitcoin ecosystem in any way, including miners, bitcoin exchanges, bitcoin funds, and investment banks. If gambling licenses are required, at minimum the public would then understand what trading in bitcoin really is and the result would likely negatively impact the price of bitcoin. At maximum, the direct government oversight, transparency, gambling-specific taxation and other regulations required by the gambling licenses in major jurisdictions in the world would likely destroy trust in bitcoin and precipitate a collapse in the bitcoin network and price.

Gambling regulators must immediately take action to investigate under their existing regulations before there is more damage to the public.

11.5. The waste of resources

The bitcoin network wastes huge amounts of electricity. Today, the whole bitcoin system consumes in a year as much energy as Venezuela consumes in a year. The electricity and computer equipment (chips) have alternative use in other sectors. The vast mining creates large negative externalities on other sectors in terms of higher prices and shortages for both electricity and chips.

Since the bitcoin system does not produce any output – not even taxes specifically due from gambling to governments – that is useful for society, but has vast negative externalities on other sectors, the societal value is negative. Bitcoin is less than worthless.

11.6. A social construct must be understandable to most people

However, it is not all bad. Most people are rational. It is not only the number of bitcoin which has a limit, but also the number of people who participate in open Ponzi schemes or gambling. The technobabble that distracts from the non-functions of bitcoin also sets a limit. Few people are willing to adopt, or to invest in, something that they do not understand. Jack Weatherford explains in his book, "The History of Money", that money, assets, the system of measurements, and the calendar are social and cultural constructs that may have arbitrary aspects; for example, the calendar can be based on the movements of the sun, the planets or the moon, or a combination of all of them. However, for these social constructs to gain a foothold in society, they need to be stable, predictable and have an anchor in the real world – and they must at least be understandable to the ordinary citizen on the street.

Bitcoin is not.

Appendix A

Department of Justice
Office of Public Affairs

FOR IMMEDIATE RELEASE
Thursday, October 8, 2020

Attorney General William P. Barr Announces Publication of Cryptocurrency Enforcement Framework

Attorney General William P. Barr announced today the release of "Cryptocurrency: An Enforcement Framework," a publication produced by the Attorney General's Cyber-Digital Task Force. The Framework provides a comprehensive overview of the emerging threats and enforcement challenges associated with the increasing prevalence and use of cryptocurrency; details the important relationships that the Department of Justice has built with regulatory and enforcement partners both within the United States government and around the world; and outlines the Department's response strategies.

"Cryptocurrency is a technology that could fundamentally transform how human beings interact, and how we organize society. Ensuring that use of this technology is safe, and does not imperil our public safety or our national security, is vitally important to America and its allies," said Attorney General Barr. "I am grateful to the Cyber-Digital Task Force for producing this detailed report, which provides a cohesive, first-of-its kind framework for those seeking to understand federal enforcement priorities in this growing space."

"At the FBI, we see first-hand the dangers posed when criminals bend the important technological promise of cryptocurrency to illicit ends," said FBI Director Christopher Wray. "As this Enforcement Framework describes, we see criminals using cryptocurrency to try to prevent us from 'following the money' across a wide range of investigations, as well as to trade in illicit goods like criminal tools on the dark web. For example, the cyber criminals behind ransomware attacks often use cryptocurrency to try to hide their true identities when acquiring malware and infrastructure, and receiving ransom payments. The men and women of the FBI are constantly innovating to keep pace with the evolution of criminals' use of cryptocurrency."

"The United States has been enormously successful blocking terrorists, rogue regimes, and their supporters from funding their activity using traditional currencies," said Task Force member John C. Demers, Assistant Attorney General for the National Security Division. "As the Cryptocurrency Enforcement Framework explains, we will adapt our strategy and tools to 21st century financing, including to combat the use of cryptocurrencies to evade enforcement and harm our national security."

119

"Cryptocurrencies and distributed ledger technology present tremendous promise for the future, but it is critical that these important innovations follow the law. The Cryptocurrency Enforcement Framework provides the public with important information intended to help them understand and comply with their obligations under the legal regimes that govern these new and fast-developing technologies," said Task Force member Brian C. Rabbitt, the acting Assistant Attorney General for the Criminal Division. "While the Department of Justice and its partners are committed to supporting the advancement of legitimate cryptocurrency technologies and uses, we will not hesitate to enforce the laws that govern these technologies when necessary to protect the public."

Task Force member Beth A. Williams, who serves as Assistant Attorney General for the Office of Legal Policy, lauded the release of the Cryptocurrency Enforcement Framework: "The Department of Justice is committed to protecting the public from current and emerging cyber threats, including those involving cryptocurrency and related technologies. This Framework reflects the Department's extensive cooperation with domestic and international partners in ensuring that we are adequately addressing these challenges, to the benefit of lawful cryptocurrency users and the public at large."

The Enforcement Framework opens with an introductory essay authored by the Task Force's chair, Associate Deputy Attorney General Sujit Raman.

Then, in Part I, the Framework provides a detailed threat overview, cataloging the three categories into which most illicit uses of cryptocurrency typically fall: (1) financial transactions associated with the commission of crimes; (2) money laundering and the shielding of legitimate activity from tax, reporting, or other legal requirements; and (3) crimes, such as theft, directly implicating the cryptocurrency marketplace itself.

Part II explores the various legal and regulatory tools at the government's disposal to confront the threats posed by cryptocurrency's illicit uses, and highlights the strong and growing partnership between the Department of Justice and the Securities and Exchange Commission, the Commodity Futures Commission, and agencies within the Department of the Treasury, among others, to enforce federal law in the cryptocurrency space.

Finally, the Enforcement Framework concludes in Part III with a discussion of the ongoing challenges the government faces in cryptocurrency enforcement – particularly with respect to business models (employed by certain cryptocurrency exchanges, platforms, kiosks, and casinos), and to activity (like "mixing" and "tumbling," "chain hopping," and certain instances of jurisdictional arbitrage) that may facilitate criminal activity.

The Cryptocurrency Enforcement Framework is the second detailed report issued by the Attorney General's Cyber-Digital Task Force, which was established in February 2018 to answer two basic questions: How is the Department of Justice responding to global cyber threats? And how can federal law enforcement accomplish its mission in this area more effectively? An earlier Task Force report, published in July 2018, canvassed a wide spectrum of cyber threats, ranging from transnational criminal enterprises' sophisticated cyber-enabled schemes, to malign foreign influence operations, to efforts to compromise our nation's critical infrastructure, and articulated the Department's priorities in detecting, deterring, and disrupting cyber threats.

Additional Cyber-Digital Task Force members include Andrew E. Lelling, United States Attorney for the District of Massachusetts, and two senior FBI executives. Components from across the Department contributed to the Cryptocurrency Enforcement Framework's drafting.

Bob Seeman and Roger Svensson

Appendix B

Department of Justice
Office of Public Affairs

FOR IMMEDIATE RELEASE
Tuesday, January 12, 2021

Owner of Bitcoin Exchange Sentenced to Prison for Money Laundering

A Bulgarian national who was convicted by a federal jury for his role in a transnational and multimillion-dollar scheme to defraud American victims was sentenced today to 121 months in prison.

Acting Assistant Attorney General David P. Burns of the Justice Department's Criminal Division, U.S. Attorney Robert M. Duncan Jr. of the Eastern District of Kentucky, and Resident Agent in Charge John Oldham of the U.S. Secret Service made the announcement.

U.S. District Court Judge Robert E. Weir sentenced Rossen G. Iossifov, 53, formerly of Bulgaria, for conspiracy to commit a Racketeer Influenced and Corrupt Organizations Act (RICO) offense and conspiracy to commit money laundering.

According to trial evidence, Iossifov owned and managed RG Coins, a cryptocurrency exchange headquartered in Sofia, Bulgaria. According to the evidence at trial, Iossifov knowingly and intentionally engaged in business practices designed to both assist fraudsters in laundering the proceeds of their fraud and to shield himself from criminal liability. At least five of Iossifov's principal clients in Bulgaria were Romanian scammers, who belonged to a criminal enterprise known in court records as the Alexandria (Romania) Online Auction Fraud (AOAF) Network.

More specifically, according to court documents and evidence presented at trial, Iossifov and his co-conspirators participated in a criminal conspiracy that engaged in a large-scale scheme of online auction fraud that victimized at least 900 Americans. Romania-based members of the conspiracy posted false advertisements to popular online auction and sales websites – such as craigslist and eBay – for high-cost goods (typically vehicles) that did not actually exist. Once victims were convinced to send payment, the conspiracy engaged in a complicated money laundering scheme wherein domestic associates would accept victim funds, convert these funds to cryptocurrency, and transfer proceeds in the form of cryptocurrency to foreign-based money launderers. Iossifov was one such foreign-based money launderer who facilitated this final step in the scheme.

According to evidence at trial, Iossifov designed his business to cater to criminal enterprises by, for instance, providing more favorable exchange rates to members of the AOAF Network. Iossifov also allowed his criminal clients to conduct cryptocurrency exchanges for cash without requiring any identification or documentation to show the source of funds, despite his representations to the contrary to the major bitcoin exchanges that supported his business. Evidence submitted during trial and his sentencing hearing revealed that Iossifov laundered nearly $5 million in cryptocurrency for four of these five scammers in a period of less than three years. This represented over $7 million in funds defrauded from American victims. In return, Iossifov made over $184,000 in proceeds from these transactions.

Iossifov was convicted after a two-week trial in front of Judge Weir in Frankfort, Kentucky in September 2020.

Under federal law, Iossifov must serve 85 percent of his prison sentence.

Thus far, 17 members of the AOAF Network have been convicted for their role in this scheme, including Iossifov. Seven others have been sentenced, including Livui-Sorin Nedelcu to 82 months in prison, Marius Dorin Cernat to 50 months in prison, Stefan Alexandru Paiusi to 31 months in prison, Eugen Alin Badea to 40 months in prison, Florin Arvat to 30 months in prison, Alin Ionut Dobric to 37 months in prison, and Austin Edward Nedved to 96 months in prison. Three members are fugitives.

The investigation was conducted by the U.S. Secret Service, Kentucky State Police, Lexington Police Department, IRS Criminal Investigation and U.S. Postal Inspection Service, and supported by the Justice Department's Organized Crime Drug Enforcement Task Force (OCDETF) and the International Organized Crime Intelligence and Operations Center (IOC-2). Assistance was provided by the Romanian National Police (Service for Combating Cybercrime), the Romanian Directorate for Investigating Organized Crime and Terrorism (Agency for Prosecuting Organized Crime), and the Supreme Prosecutor's Office of Cassation of the Republic of Bulgaria. The Justice Department's Office of International Affairs and Money Laundering and Asset Recovery Section of the Criminal Division provided significant support. This case is being prosecuted by Senior Counsel Frank Lin and Senior Trial Attorney Timothy Flowers of the Criminal Division's Computer Crime and Intellectual Property Section and Assistant U.S. Attorneys Kathryn M. Anderson and Kenneth R. Taylor of the U.S. Attorney's Office for the Eastern District of Kentucky.

Individuals believing they may be victims of the advanced fee and online auction fraud or brute-force attack schemes described herein are encouraged to visit the following website to obtain more information: https://justice.gov/usao-edky/information-victims-large-cases.

Bitcoin: Unlicensed Gambling

Bob Seeman and Roger Svensson

Appendix C

Department of Justice
Office of Public Affairs

FOR IMMEDIATE RELEASE
Wednesday, May 5, 2021

Court Authorizes Service of John Doe Summons Seeking Identities of U.S. Taxpayers Who Have Used Cryptocurrency

A federal court in the Northern District of California entered an order today authorizing the IRS to serve a John Doe summons on Payward Ventures Inc., and Subsidiaries d/b/a Kraken (Kraken) seeking information about U.S. taxpayers who conducted at least the equivalent of $20,000 in transactions in cryptocurrency during the years 2016 to 2020. The IRS is seeking the records of Americans who engaged in business with or through Kraken, a digital currency exchanger headquartered in San Francisco, California.

"Gathering the information in the summons approved today is an important step to ensure cryptocurrency owners are following the tax laws," said Acting Assistant Attorney General David A. Hubbert of the Justice Department's Tax Division. "Those who transact with cryptocurrency must meet their tax obligations like any other taxpayer."

"There is no excuse for taxpayers continuing to fail to report the income earned and taxes due from virtual currency transactions," said IRS Commissioner Chuck Rettig. "This John Doe summons is part of our effort to uncover those who are trying to skirt reporting and avoid paying their fair share."

Cryptocurrency, as generally defined, is a digital representation of value. Because transactions in cryptocurrencies can be difficult to trace and have an inherently pseudoanonymous aspect, taxpayers may be using them to hide taxable income from the IRS. On April 1, 2021, a federal court in the District of Massachusetts granted an order authorizing the IRS to serve a similar John Doe summons on Circle, a digital currency exchange headquartered in Boston.

Today's order from the Northern District of California grants the IRS permission to serve what is known as a "John Doe" summons on Kraken. The United States' petition does not allege that Kraken has engaged in any wrongdoing in connection with its digital currency exchange business. Rather, according to the court's order, the summons seeks information related to the IRS's "investigation of an ascertainable group or class of persons" that the IRS has reasonable basis to believe "may have failed to comply with internal revenue laws." According to the copy of the summons filed with the petition, the IRS directed Kraken to produce records identifying the U.S. taxpayers described above, along with other documents relating to their cryptocurrency transactions.

The IRS has issued guidance regarding the tax consequences on the use of virtual currencies in IRS Notice 2014-21, which provides that virtual currencies that can be converted into traditional currency are property for tax purposes, and a taxpayer can have a gain or loss on the sale or exchange of a virtual currency, depending on the taxpayer's cost to purchase the virtual currency (that is, the taxpayer's tax basis).

Appendix D

U.S. Commodity Futures Trading Commission

Customer Advisory: Understand the Risks of Virtual Currency Trading

The U.S. Commodity Futures Trading Commission (CFTC) is issuing this customer advisory to inform the public of possible risks associated with investing or speculating in virtual currencies or recently launched Bitcoin futures and options.

Virtual currency is a digital representation of value that functions as a medium of exchange, a unit of account, or a store of value, but it does not have legal tender status. Virtual currencies are sometimes exchanged for U.S. dollars or other currencies around the world, but they are not currently backed nor supported by any government or central bank. Their value is completely derived by market forces of supply and demand, and they are more volatile than traditional fiat currencies. Profits and losses related to this volatility are amplified in margined futures contracts.

Bitcoin is a Commodity

Bitcoin and other virtual currencies have been determined to be commodities under the Commodity Exchange Act (CEA). The Commission primarily regulates commodity derivatives contracts that are based on underlying commodities. While its regulatory oversight authority over commodity cash markets is limited, the CFTC maintains general anti-fraud and manipulation enforcement authority over virtual currency cash markets as a commodity in interstate commerce.

For hedgers – those who own Bitcoin or other virtual currencies and who are looking to protect themselves against potential losses or looking to buy virtual currencies at some point in the future – futures contracts and options are intended to provide protection against this volatility. However, like all futures products, speculating in these markets should be considered a high-risk transaction.

What makes virtual currency risky?

Purchasing virtual currencies on the cash market – spending dollars to purchase Bitcoin for your personal wallet, for example – comes with a number of risks, including:

- Most cash markets are not regulated or supervised by a government agency;
- Platforms in the cash market may lack critical system safeguards, including customer protections;
- Volatile cash market price swings or flash crashes;
- Cash market manipulation;
- Cyber risks, such as hacking customer wallets; and/or
- Platforms selling from their own accounts and putting customers at an unfair disadvantage.

It's also important to note that market changes that affect the cash market price of a virtual currency may ultimately affect the price of virtual currency futures and options.

When customers purchase a virtual currency-based futures contract, they may not be entitled to receive the actual virtual currency, depending on the particular contract. Under most futures contracts currently being offered, customers are buying the right to receive or pay the amount of an underlying commodity value in dollars at some point in the future. Such futures contracts are said to be "cash settled." Customers will pay or receive (depending on which side of the contract they have taken – long or short) the dollar equivalent of the virtual currency based on an index or auction price specified in the contract. Thus, customers should inform themselves as to how the index or auction prices used to settle the contract are determined.

Entering into futures contracts through leveraged accounts can amplify the risks of trading the product. Typically, participants only fund futures contracts at a fraction of the underlying commodity price when using a margin account. This creates "leverage," and leverage amplifies the underlying risk, making a change in the cash price even more significant. When prices move in the customers' favor, leverage provides them with more profit for a relatively small investment. But, when markets go against customers' positions, they will be forced to refill their margin accounts or close out their positions, and in the end may lose more than their initial investments.

Beware of related fraud

Virtual currencies are commonly targeted by hackers and criminals who commit fraud. There is no assurance of recourse if your virtual currency is stolen. Be careful how and where you store your virtual currency. The CFTC has received complaints about virtual currency exchange scams, as well as Ponzi and "pyramid" schemes.

- If you decide to buy virtual currencies or derivatives based on them, remember these tips:
- If someone tries to sell you an investment in options or futures on virtual currencies, including Bitcoin, verify they are registered with the CFTC.
- Remember—much of the virtual currency cash market operates through Internet-based trading platforms that may be unregulated and unsupervised.
- Do not invest in products or strategies you do not understand.
- Be sure you understand the risks and how the product can lose money, as well as the likelihood of loss. Only speculate with money you can afford to lose.
- There is no such thing as a guaranteed investment or trading strategy. If someone tells you there is no risk of losing money, do not invest.
- Investors should conduct extensive research into the legitimacy of virtual currency platforms and digital wallets before providing credit card information, wiring money, or offering sensitive personal information.
- The SEC has also warned that some token sales or initial coin offerings (ICOs) can be used to improperly entice investors with promises of high returns.

Appendix E

Commodity Futures Trading Commission

Release Number 8371-21

Federal Court Orders UK Man to Pay More Than $571 Million for Operating Fraudulent Bitcoin Trading Scheme

March 26, 2021

Washington, D.C. — The Commodity Futures Trading Commission today announced that the U.S. District Court for the Southern District of New York entered a default judgment against **Benjamin Reynolds**, purportedly of Manchester, England, finding that he operated a fraudulent scheme to solicit bitcoin from members of the public and misappropriated customers' bitcoin. This case was brought in connection with the Division of Enforcement's Digital Assets Task Force.

The court's March 2, 2021 order requires Reynolds to pay nearly $143 million in restitution to defrauded customers and a civil monetary penalty of $429 million. The order also permanently enjoins Reynolds from engaging in conduct that violates the Commodity Exchange Act and CFTC regulations, registering with the CFTC, and trading in any CFTC-regulated markets.

The judgment is the result of a 2019 enforcement action brought by the CFTC charging Reynolds, conducting business as Control-Finance Limited, with fraud and misappropriation. [See CFTC Press Release No. 7938-19]

Case Background

Between May 2017 and October 2017, Reynolds used a public website, various social media accounts, and email communications to solicit at least 22,190.542 bitcoin, valued at approximately $143 million at the time, from more than 1,000 customers worldwide, including at least 169 individuals residing in the U.S.

Among other things, Reynolds falsely represented to customers that Control-Finance traded their bitcoin deposits in virtual currency markets and employed specialized virtual currency traders who generated guaranteed trading profits for all customers. He also constructed an elaborate affiliate marketing network that relied on fraudulently promising to pay outsized referral profits, rewards, and bonuses to encourage customers to refer new customers to Control-Finance. In fact, Reynolds made no trades on customers' behalf, earned no trading profits for them, and paid them no referral rewards or bonuses. While Reynolds represented that he would return all bitcoin deposits to customers of Control-Finance by late October 2017, he never did and instead retained the deposits for his own personal use. Customers lost most or all of their bitcoin deposits as a result of the scheme.

The CFTC cautions victims that restitution orders may not result in the recovery of any money lost because the wrongdoers may not have sufficient funds or assets. The CFTC will continue to fight vigorously for the protection of customers and to ensure wrongdoers are held accountable.

Appendix F

U.S. Department of the Treasury

The Financial Crimes Enforcement Network Proposes Rule Aimed at Closing Anti-Money Laundering Regulatory Gaps for Certain Convertible Virtual Currency and Digital Asset Transactions

December 18, 2020

The Financial Crimes Enforcement Network (FinCEN), a bureau within the U.S. Department of the Treasury, is requesting comments on proposed requirements for certain transactions involving convertible virtual currency (CVC) or digital assets with legal tender status (LTDA). Under the Notice of Proposed Rulemaking (NPRM) submitted to the Federal Register today, banks and money services businesses (MSBs) would be required to submit reports, keep records, and verify the identity of customers in relation to transactions above certain thresholds involving CVC/LTDA wallets not hosted by a financial institution (also known as "unhosted wallets") or CVC/LTDA wallets hosted by a financial institution in certain jurisdictions identified by FinCEN.

The United States welcomes responsible innovation, including new technologies that may improve the efficiency of the financial system and expand access to financial services. Today's action seeks to protect national security and aid law enforcement by increasing transparency in digital currencies and closing loopholes that malign actors may exploit.

"This rule addresses substantial national security concerns in the CVC market, and aims to close the gaps that malign actors seek to exploit in the recordkeeping and reporting regime," said Secretary Steven T. Mnuchin. "The rule, which applies to financial institutions and is consistent with existing requirements, is intended to protect national security, assist law enforcement, and increase transparency while minimizing impact on responsible innovation."

The proposed rule complements existing BSA requirements applicable to banks and MSBs by proposing to add reporting requirements for CVC and LTDA transactions exceeding $10,000 in value. Pursuant to the proposed rule, banks and MSBs will have 15 days from the date on which a reportable transaction occurs to file a report with FinCEN. Further, this proposed rule would require banks and MSBs to keep records of a customer's CVC or LTDA transactions and counterparties, including verifying the identity of their customers, if a counterparty uses an unhosted or otherwise covered wallet and the transaction is greater than $3,000.

This includes collecting the following:

1. The name and address of the financial institution's customer;

2. The type of CVC or LTDA used in the transaction;

3. The amount of CVC or LTDA in the transaction;

4. The time of the transaction;

5. The assessed value of the transaction, in U.S. Dollars, based on the prevailing exchange rate at the time of the transaction;

6. Any payment instructions received from the financial institution's customer;

7. The name and physical address of each counterparty to the transaction of the financial institution's customer;

8. Other counterparty information the Secretary may prescribe as mandatory on the reporting form for transactions subject to reporting pursuant to § 1010.316(b);

9. Any other information that uniquely identifies the transaction, the accounts, and, to the extent reasonably available, the parties involved; and,

10. Any form relating to the transaction that is completed or signed by the financial institution's customer.

Appendix G

Investor.gov

U.S. SECURITIES AND EXCHANGE COMMISSION

Thinking About Buying the Latest New Cryptocurrency or Token?

By Lori Schock, Director of the SEC's Office of Investor Education and Advocacy

Should you or shouldn't you buy the latest new cryptocurrency or token? I can't tell you how many people have come up to me and asked if they should invest in bitcoin. I recently conducted an investor education program at a retirement community and a woman said to me, "My children keep telling me I need to hurry up and invest in bitcoin—is it safe, have I already missed the boat?" Seniors are not the only ones interested in bitcoin and other cryptocurrency-related investments. Millennials are also jumping on the bandwagon. While I can't give investment advice about bitcoin or any other cryptocurrency-related investment or product, I can provide advice on some things you should consider when deciding if an investment is right for you.

Perhaps the most important thing to know is the cryptocurrency-related investment markets are very different than our regulated securities markets. For example, our securities laws provide important protections that you may not be getting when dealing in cryptocurrency-related investments. In many cases you may not know exactly who you are dealing with, where your money is going or what you are getting in return. For more detailed information, you can check out SEC Chairman Jay Clayton's statement on cryptocurrencies and initial coin offerings (ICOs) and the Office of Investor Education and Advocacy's investor bulletin on ICOs.

These digital assets have been trending and receiving the attention of celebrities, often through endorsements. You may see them on social media, radio or TV promoting bitcoin and a variety of other products and services. Never make an investment decision based solely on celebrity endorsements. Just because your favorite celebrity says a product or service is a good investment doesn't mean it is. Always do thorough, independent research of the product.

Trendy investments are especially ripe for fraudsters so be aware there is a real risk of fraud. Scam artists prey upon the newness of an investment opportunity when there isn't as much history about the product. It's also easier to sell an investor on an "everyone is buying it" sales pitch when there's a lot of buzz about a certain investment product. The pressure to buy the product right away mounts.

Don't fall for high-pressure sales tactics, the promise of guaranteed returns or too good to be true claims. You should check out the red flags of investment fraud on Investor.gov as well as check to see if the investment professional you're dealing with is registered. Take time to make the right investment decision for you. Ask questions and demand clear answers. You can find sample questions, such as "Who exactly am I contracting with?" and "What will my money be used for?" here.

You should understand if you lose money there is a real chance the SEC and other regulators won't be able to help you recover your investment, even in cases of fraud.

If you do choose to purchase digital currencies or tokens, recognize that they are new. There may be significant risk involved in putting your money into something that hasn't been around very long. A good rule of thumb when investing in a new product is to only invest money that you are willing to lose, so that it's not financially devastating if the investment doesn't pan out. One way to spread risk is to diversify your investments. Don't put all of your eggs in one basket. That way, if one of your investments loses money, the other investments can make up for it.

Cryptocurrencies may be today's shiny, new opportunity but there are serious risks involved. Proceed with caution, do your research, evaluate your financial goals and most importantly, don't flip a coin when you're making investment decisions. Before you invest, go to Investor.gov to learn how to invest wisely and avoid fraud.

Appendix H

United States Marshal

FOR SALE
Approximately 4,041.58424932 bitcoin

THIS NOTICE DOES NOT CONSTITUTE AN OFFER TO SELL BUT INVITES INTERESTED PARTIES TO SUBMIT A BID FOR PURCHASE. THE FOLLOWING INFORMATION IS BEING PROVIDED WITHOUT RECOURSE TO THE UNITED STATES OF AMERICA AND THE UNITED STATES MARSHALS SERVICE.

CHECK BACK FREQUENTLY FOR UPDATES

PLEASE READ ALL INSTRUCTIONS CAREFULLY.

FAILURE TO COMPLY WITH ANY OF THE FOLLOWING INSTRUCTIONS WILL RESULT IN DISQUALIFICATION FROM THIS SEALED BID AUCTION.

This sealed bid auction is for 4,041.58424932 Bitcoin (structure details below). The required deposit to participate in this auction is $200,000.00 USD.

These Bitcoin were forfeited in various federal criminal, civil and administrative cases, including:

United States v. Tyler Lee Ward et al., (Case No. 18-cr-438)

DEA Administrative Forfeiture of 1.3766326 Bitcoin

DEA Administrative Forfeiture of 4.94507746 Bitcoin

DEA Administrative Forfeiture of 7.13218 Bitcoin

DEA Administrative Forfeiture of 1.49273858 Bitcoin

DEA Administrative Forfeiture of 14.95978524 Bitcoin

United States v. Ryan Farace (Case No. 18-cr-00018)

United States v. Matthew Lee Yensan (Case No. 17-cr-00303)

DEA Administrative Forfeiture of 1.65659480 Bitcoin

DEA Administrative Forfeiture of 0.66224525 Bitcoin

DEA Administrative Forfeiture of 14.59638483 Bitcoin

DEA Administrative Forfeiture of 0.24130732 Bitcoin

DEA Administrative Forfeiture of 104.34765685 Bitcoin

United States v. Alexandre Cazes, et al., (Case No. 17-cv-00967)

FBI Administrative Forfeiture of 3.33369 Bitcoin

United States v. Ronald L. Wheeler, III (Case No. 17-cr-377)

United States v. Konrads Voits (Case No. 17-cr-20689)

FBI Administrative Forfeiture of 535 Bitcoin

HSI-USCBP Administrative Forfeiture of 0.82609561 Bitcoin

HSI-USCBP Administrative Forfeiture of 8.91 Bitcoin

HSI-USCBP Administrative Forfeiture of Jaxx Wallet BTC (approximately 0.232 btc)

HSI-USCBP Administrative Forfeiture of 0.27698615 Bitcoin

HSI-USCBP Administrative Forfeiture of BITCOINS (approximately 3.544 btc)

HSI-USCBP Administrative Forfeiture of 26.3765293 Bitcoin

HSI-USCBP Administrative Forfeiture of 17.49013698 Bitcoin

HSI-USCBP Administrative Forfeiture of 1.75799537 Bitcoin and 3.63951363 Bitcoin

HSI-USCBP Administrative Forfeiture of 22.89799376 Bitcoin

HSI-USCBP Administrative Forfeiture of 2.02903322 Bitcoin

HSI-USCBP Administrative Forfeiture of 24.21055495 Bitcoin

Appendix I

Department of Justice
Journal of Federal Law and Practice

May 20, 2021

Surfing the First Wave of Cryptocurrency Money Laundering

Alexandra D. Comolli
Management and Program Analyst
Money Laundering, Forfeiture, and Bank Fraud Unit Federal Bureau of Investigation

Michele R. Korver
Digital Currency Counsel
Criminal Division
Money Laundering and Asset Recovery Section

"You can't stop the waves, but you can learn to surf."

I. Introduction: a revolution—and a gnarly wave—unleashed

Bitcoin was unveiled to the world in January 2009. Its pseudonymous creator, Satoshi Nakamoto, pieced together this creation with cryptography, systems engineering, and economics. He, she, or they designed a self-sustaining distributed system that would allow individuals to exchange value without a centralized arbiter. In other words, an internet of value. Nakamoto's vision is now reality. Value can be transferred around the world, ad infinitum, without ever touching a financial institution. While this is likely a revolutionary technology, it also created new money laundering risks.

For practitioners working in areas that touch upon cryptocurrency, this article describes what the first wave of cryptocurrency money laundering looks like, discusses what regulations and laws apply to such conduct, and touches on some emerging business models and techniques that will likely drive the second and third waves of cryptocurrency money laundering.

As described below, cryptocurrency-related money laundering has followed the traditional placement, layering, and integration model, but it does so with a new set of technologies and gatekeepers.

II. Why cryptocurrency is a unique money laundering tool

The history of Bitcoin and other cryptocurrencies has been thoroughly covered in academic literature and, therefore, is not covered here. For the purposes of this article, the following features of cryptocurrencies—and their underlying blockchains—are most important:

- They are decentralized;
- they are pseudonymous;
- they are immutable; and
- their ledgers may be transparent or opaque.

But before delving into these features, we need a primary definition. Cryptocurrency, a type of virtual currency, is a decentralized peer-to-peer network-based medium of value or exchange. Cryptocurrency may be used as a substitute for government-backed "fiat" currency to buy goods or services or exchanged for fiat currency or other cryptocurrencies. Early virtual currencies, like E-Gold, facilitated substantial money laundering, but for the reasons explained below, did not create a new paradigm for transferring value. Rather, they were centralized and depended on an institution to clear transactions. Accordingly, when those institutions broke bad, they were shut down like any other dirty financial institution. As explained below, cryptocurrency is a paradigm shift that permanently changed the money laundering landscape.

A. Decentralized

Cryptocurrencies are decentralized in that the processing and confirmation of transactions takes place through users and not through a centralized authority, such as a bank. In avoiding a centralized authority, cryptocurrencies can, at least in theory, allow individuals to move funds without interacting with a regulated gatekeeper, such as a depository institution or a money services business. Accordingly, in the traditional typology of money laundering, cryptocurrencies allow criminals to breeze through the placement and layering stages, though as described below, the integration stage remains a major obstacle—largely because cryptocurrency is not yet a widely adopted means of payment for goods and services.

Decentralization also means that there may not be a centralized institution to prosecute if a cryptocurrency is used for illegal purposes. Even though individuals and coding committees are responsible for continually updating a cryptocurrency's code, that body usually is not responsible for confirming individual transactions and, thus, is not in the same position as, for instance, the principals of E-Gold. The lines may become more blurred, however, in the context of decentralized exchanges, where the purpose of the software is to facilitate money transmission, and the owners of such software make a commission on those transactions.

B. Pseudonymous

Pseudonymity is the partially anonymous state in which a user maintains consistent identifiers—in this case, wallet addresses—that are different from the user's official identifiers, such as a name and social security number. For a cryptocurrency blockchain to confirm transactions, it must be able to verify inputs and outputs to and from wallet addresses. As such, even if an individual uses a different address for every transaction, the historical trail from the present, Z, to the past, A, will be transactionally connected. This means that, if law enforcement can tie wallet address Z to Jane Doe, all transactions from Z to A may also have a connection to her. Thus, blockchains may, in some respects, be worse for criminals than cash because any operational security failure may allow all their transactions to be linked to them—whereas cash has no ledger associated with it. Nonetheless, even with this risk, cryptocurrencies allow criminals to digitally transact without providing standard identification information to a regulated gatekeeper—much like individuals exchanging cash in-person.

C. Transparent

Closely related to pseudonymity is whether a blockchain is transparent. This feature is often confused with the public/private distinction, but it is in fact different. A blockchain can be any combination of these four features. The public/private feature of a blockchain refers to who has permission to use it. In other words, a public blockchain is one that anyone can transact in and, thus, does not require special permissions, whereas a private blockchain limits access to specific users (and is often used by a single company or conglomeration). Conversely, the transparency of a blockchain refers to who can observe it.

In the context of cryptocurrency, a transparent blockchain, such as the Bitcoin blockchain, allows the public to see the entire history of every transaction ever conducted on it. By contrast, an opaque blockchain, such as the types employed by so-called anonymity or privacy-enhanced coins, prevent the public from seeing the source, amount, or destination of any transaction. Transparent blockchains hold two main advantages: First, they often operate more efficiently because transactions carry less technical layers of obfuscation technology, and second, they are more easily adaptable for applications beyond cryptocurrency. A third and more speculative benefit is that transparent blockchains lack the risk factors associated with privacy coins that either overtly or functionally cater to the criminal element. A combination of these three factors is likely the reason why privacy coins are less widely used.

In the context of money laundering, opaque blockchains are more problematic. As noted above, transparent blockchains allow law enforcement to connect the dots between transactions. If Jane Doe is found to be the user of wallet Z, then in theory, the entire history of the inputs into that wallet can be discovered—not so on opaque blockchains. Monero, for example, uses ring signatures that mix inputs to obscure their historical trails. Yet, it appears unlikely that the technology underpinning privacy coins will win the arms race against crypto-investigative companies. Even so, opaque blockchains will continue to add another layer of frustration to those attempting to trace cryptocurrency transactions.

D. Immutable

Blockchains are immutable because the verification of present time transaction Z depends on its historical antecedents. In other words, you cannot confirm a transaction if it does not correspond to all prior transactions in its history. The immutability of blockchains is what makes them a likely source of highly useful applications unrelated to cryptocurrency. In more concrete terms, a block in a blockchain is equivalent to a photo of someone holding up the front page of the New York Times, which reveals that the photo could not have been taken on a later date than what is printed on the paper. But unlike a photo, which can be doctored, each transaction on a blockchain has a unique hash, which proves it is the legitimate successor to all previous transactions on the blockchain. Any change to the content of those transactions results in a different, illegitimate hash.

Useful applications can be built into blockchains because of this feature, including smart contracts, identity verification, and restricted data storage. For law enforcement, the immutability of blockchains is advantageous. The immutability of blockchains means that the data contained in them is tamper-proof. As such, if a criminal can be tied to transactions on a blockchain, she cannot claim that they were fake. Relatedly, blockchains are easy to authenticate at trial, even without a custodian of records. While prosecutors may choose to call a subject-matter expert to explain how blockchains work and to present the specific transactions at issue, the data itself doesn't need further authentication because it is confirmed by the system itself. In sum, immutability is a feature of blockchains that benefits law enforcement and the accused, if using blockchain evidence as a defense.

III. Money laundering 101: placement, layering, and integration

Rather than abstractly defining money laundering, it makes more sense to describe the purpose it serves. At its core, money laundering is about making dirty money usable. "Money-laundering . . . [is] the process of trying to disguise illicit-profits in order to enjoy the use of all ascribed legitimate, standardised and commonly shared agentive functions of money while the criminal origins of the entity incorporating these functions (money) are hidden." The process of money laundering is traditionally divided into three stages: placement, layering, and integration (PLI). This schema makes sense but rarely applies neatly to any specific money laundering scheme.

Briefly, placement is getting the dirty proceeds into or through a gatekeeping institution, such as a bank, money services business (MSB), or informal value transfer system (such as hawala). Once placed into one of these institutions, a criminal can begin carrying out transactions to obscure the source, nature, ownership, or control of the proceeds. Layering can involve wire transfers, ACHs, person-to-person handoffs, and in the context of cryptocurrency, movement of funds from various wallet addresses (often done through mixing and tumbling services). The final broad stage of money laundering is integration, in which the proceeds are blended into the criminal's existing life to make them potentially undetectable. For example, placement occurs when a criminal takes laundered funds out of front accounts to purchase luxury items like vehicles and real property. Once purchased, the vehicles and real property can be described as integrated into the criminal's financial holdings, thus completing the PLI cycle.

Different money laundering techniques are associated with different parts of the PLI process. For example, structuring, in which a criminal manipulates cash deposits to prevent a gatekeeper from filing a mandated report—such as a Currency Transaction Report or (CTR)— is typically part of the placement stage. Likewise, intricate conversions of proceeds to other forms of value, such as from cash to electronic funds to precious metals and back to cash, are part of the layering phase. As described in detail below, cryptocurrency money laundering often follows the PLI model, but sometimes at a faster pace, particularly in the layering phase. This is largely because of the decentralized nature of cryptocurrency, which allows transactions to be made quickly and globally without using a trusted third party that would be obligated to carry out due diligence on customers and transactions.

Before examining how cryptocurrency money laundering looks through the prism of the PLI model, it is helpful to first understand the most common crimes involving cryptocurrency. As described in more detail below, the typical flow of funds in cryptocurrency money laundering is from cryptocurrency to fiat currency. This movement occurs because criminals may obtain ill-gotten funds in the form of cryptocurrency and need to make it usable by converting it to fiat currency and other tangible assets. Dark web commerce illustrates how the flow of funds move from cryptocurrency to fiat currency. In this ecosystem, vendors of illegal goods and services are paid in cryptocurrency because no institutional payment processors, such as Visa or Mastercard, will allow their services to be used on dark web marketplaces. Vendors of narcotics, hacking tools, stolen personally identifiable information, and illegal services often end up with bulks of cryptocurrency that need to be converted into fiat currency, which can be used to buy tangible goods or reinvested into an illegal enterprise.

The same flow of funds from cryptocurrency to fiat currency appears outside of dark web commerce. For example, ransomware attackers almost always collect their payments in cryptocurrency. They do this for many reasons, including the certainty and transparency of the payment method and the ability to quickly layer the victim's funds. The same flow of funds occurs when an institutional exchange is hacked. The attackers gain huge sums of cryptocurrency, which must be laundered and converted into fiat currency.

None of this is to say that crypto-laundering doesn't also take place in the reverse. It's possible to imagine tax cheats converting their income into cryptocurrency and then keeping the funds in that form to attempt to avoid scrutiny from tax authorities. In addition, fraudsters are increasingly converting victim funds collected in fiat to cryptocurrency to conceal the funds and attribution evidence from law enforcement, as well as to quickly and easily move the proceeds from one jurisdiction to another. Similarly, transnational criminal organizations may use P2P exchangers and other third party money launderers to convert cash proceeds of crime to cryptocurrency in order to efficiently move the funds among co-conspirators or across international borders.

With this in mind, we can first look at the placement of cryptocurrency. In one sense, placement is almost risk-free, just like when someone puts cash in a billfold. Because cryptocurrency wallets can be set up without a third-party, criminals can put funds into those wallets without any oversight. But even if wallets can be easily funded, at some point the criminal may have to place those funds into an account controlled by a regulated gatekeeper. For example, if a criminal wants to use a regulated cryptocurrency exchange, the placement of dirty crypto funds may carry the same risk as a criminal placing dirty cash into a bank. Indeed, data on cryptocurrency crime suggests that most criminal proceeds are laundered through regulated gatekeepers. If operated in a compliant manner, the cryptocurrency exchange will obtain "Know Your Customer" (KYC) information, make risk assessments, and file federally mandated reports. The criminal may circumvent this step by going through a non-compliant cryptocurrency exchange. As discussed below, regulation and enforcement has been slow to catch up with illegally operated exchanges, leaving room for criminals to easily launder their funds. Nonetheless, this advantage is temporary as cryptocurrency exchanges and service providers worldwide are increasingly being regulated to the same extent as traditional financial institutions. As such, the initial placement (of cryptocurrency into a wallet) is entirely different in the context of cryptocurrency, but the more significant step of using an intermediary entity that can actually convert the cryptocurrency into fiat currency, and vice versa, isn't much different than in the fiat world.

The second stage of layering is where criminals can take creative measures with cryptocurrency—with the risk that every transaction creates a trail that can later be traced back to them. Not having to use a third-party to conduct transactions, criminals can layer their funds by simply setting up multiple cryptocurrency addresses and having the funds sent through those addresses. This movement, sometimes called tumbling, can make it difficult to track the historical flow of funds (though the advancement of blockchain analytics has made this type of layering much less effective for criminals). Instead of sending the funds from Point A to Point B, the funds are sent through intermediary wallets for the sole purpose of creating distance from the original point of entry. These transactions likely occur without touching a regulated gatekeeper, and thus, no mandated reports such as Suspicious Activity Reports (SAR) are filed. Some may think of this as a digital hawala, but it is different in that a blockchain itself is not a regulated entity, unlike a hawala—which would be required to register as a money transmitting business and also file mandated reports with the Financial Crimes Enforcement Network (FinCEN). At the same time, every additional wallet used by a criminal is an additional breadcrumb that law enforcement can use to connect the dots of that criminal's historical conduct. Along these same lines, blockchains can also remove geographic barriers to moving funds. The possession of funds on a blockchain is based on control of a wallet's private keys. Thus, a criminal can transfer ownership simply by providing the private keys to someone else, all without ever touching a financial gatekeeper. Similarly, instead of transferring the private keys, criminals can send the value to other wallet addresses.

A wallet does not exist in a specific physical place but is, instead, just software that interacts with a blockchain. The location of the wallet is wherever control of the private keys is located. Maybe that is the location of the IP address used by the owner when trying to access the value, or maybe, in the case of cold storage wallets, it is wherever the container of the private keys is located. Just as the internet extracted information from the kinetic world, blockchains have done the same for value. The key point is that the location of the funds can be both everywhere and nowhere at the same time.

By comparison, it is useful to think through the many steps a traditional drug trafficking organization (DTO) must go through to physically move the proceeds of its endeavors from the location of distribution back to the location of manufacturing. Sometimes, DTOs use funnel accounts to geographically move funds, that is, smurfs for the DTO deposit cash at bank branches in one region and have it withdrawn in another. This is a time-consuming and risky process because financial institutions may file SARs or CTRs on the transactions—or maybe the smurfs are unreliable and steal a portion of the funds, say something stupid to the bank teller when making a transaction, or the bank closes the accounts for suspicious activity. To avoid all of this, DTOs could require their customers, or at least their lower level distributors, to pay in cryptocurrency. The funds could then be immediately transferred from one region to another, without ever touching a regulated institution. At some point, the DTO will have to convert the funds to fiat currency or some other usable form of value (the integration stage of the money laundering process), but that is a different problem for the DTO. By accepting cryptocurrency, it can potentially eliminate one of its primary money laundering concerns (though, as noted before, these transactions are still recorded on a blockchain, which leaves historical traces of all transactions for law enforcement to later analyze).

This is not to say that the placement and layering stages do not pose any risk to criminals. Several blockchain analytics companies dedicate significant resources to mapping the major blockchains. This allows users of these analytic platforms to see if funds are moving to or from illicit sources, such as wallets associated with dark web marketplaces. In theory, funds coming from dark web marketplaces could be traced to a regulated gatekeeper, such as a cryptocurrency exchange or mixing service, where law enforcement could then simply issue a subpoena for account records to the institution and work backwards from that identifying information. In other words, the mere movement of funds from an identified illicit source can pose some risk to criminals.

While cryptocurrency may provide some new money laundering techniques at the placement and layering stages, it has yet to make any changes to the traditional problems associated with integration. The key word is yet—cryptocurrency is still largely unusable at a consumer level, which means criminals must convert it to a usable form, such as fiat currency. Criminals often first encounter regulated gatekeepers at the point of conversion. They may go to a peer-to-peer (P2P) or institutional exchanger to cash out their ill- gotten cryptocurrency, but these individuals and institutions are subject to the Bank Secrecy Act and are required to maintain an anti- money laundering program and file SARs and CTRs. As discussed below, some exchangers base their business model on violating these regulations and, unsurprisingly, can charge premiums to criminals who would otherwise be screened out by compliant exchangers. Many of the crooked exchangers, however, get caught, and when this happens, their customers are discovered, as was the case with Operation Dark Gold, which is discussed below. The risks are thus unavoidable when the criminal attempts to convert her cryptocurrency to fiat. As such, until cryptocurrency becomes widely accepted at a consumer level, criminals will still be forced to integrate those funds into fiat currency, where they will encounter higher levels of risk than in the placement and layering stages.

In sum, crypto money laundering follows the general PLI model but offers some new money laundering techniques (though also with some new risks for criminals) with these new techniques. Even with the great money laundering advantages created by cryptocurrency, criminals still must convert those funds to something more usable in the fiat world. To do so, they generally must use a regulated gatekeeper. It is at this stage where any advantage for criminals is lost.

IV. The primary domains of cryptocurrency money laundering

Criminals follow common paths when placing, layering, and integrating their ill-gotten cryptocurrency. Those paths go through several primary domains, including institutional exchanges, P2P exchangers, mixing and tumbling services, and traditional banks. These paths aren't static, and it should be expected that certain emerging technologies, such as decentralized exchanges, will become a primary domain in the near future. Some of these primary domains, such as P2P exchangers and mixing services, appear to more directly cater to criminals in need of laundering cryptocurrency. With strong compliance programs, these domains carry, at best, moderate to high levels of risk. Other domains, such as institutional exchanges and depository institutions, have more legitimate bases for their business models. As such, even though they can be involved in large amounts of money laundering activity, this is a result of either high volumes of trading or weak compliance programs. But the business model itself can be justified by the existence of many non-criminal reasons why customers use the offered services. The risk for these domains, therefore, depends more on the nature of their respective compliance program and not the business model itself.

From a long-term perspective, as cryptocurrency becomes more widely adopted, it will become less likely that run-of-the-mill cryptocurrency transactions will be associated with money laundering. In the early days of cryptocurrency, a great deal of activity was tied to illegal conduct on the dark web, which is why the shuttering of dark web marketplaces could impact the value of bitcoin. But as mainstream adoption of cryptocurrency has grown, the percentage of transactions used to promote or conceal crime has also decreased. In this sense, cryptocurrency sectors not catering to money laundering, such as compliant institutional exchanges, will likely service less and less criminals as a percentage of their business. The same cannot be said for other sectors.

The various domains described below typically appear at different parts of the money laundering process. Let's discuss the examples described above, where criminals obtain their ill-gotten gains as cryptocurrency and convert it to fiat currency for use in the kinetic world. To first possess cryptocurrency, criminals must set up wallets. Those wallets might be under their exclusive control, or they might be custodial wallets hosted by a third-party service provider, such as an institutional exchange. Once in a wallet, funds can be sent to mixing services or gambling sites to obscure their historical trail. From there, the funds can be converted to fiat currency through exchanges, P2P exchangers, or kiosks. Sometimes, the funds will then be sent to bank accounts or cryptocurrency debit cards where they can be used to buy things or pay off debts. While this is the typical way in which the primary domains appear in the PLI process, criminals can use the domains in almost any way they want: Wallets can be used to mix funds; P2P exchangers can be used to integrate the funds; and kiosks can be used for layering. Criminals can also repeat the steps of the PLI process to further obfuscate the origin of the ill-gotten funds, though they incur additional costs and risk every time they repeat the cycle.

A. Wallets

Nothing can begin or end in the world of cryptocurrency without a wallet. A wallet is fundamentally the virtual equivalent of an account. Most wallets serve as an interface with blockchains and generate and store the public and private key pairs necessary to send and receive cryptocurrency. Cryptocurrency wallets can be housed in a variety of forms, including on a tangible, external device ("hardware wallets"); downloaded as software onto either a personal computer, server, or smartphone ("software wallets"); printed public and private keys ("paper wallets"); and as an online account associated with a cryptocurrency service provider such as an exchange.

1. Who holds the keys?

If the end user has sole access to the private keys, the wallet is considered non-custodial or unhosted. Hardware and paper wallets are always unhosted; they are often referred to as cold storage wallets. Alternatively, if a third-party wallet provider, such as an exchange, holds the private keys, the wallet is considered custodial or a hosted wallet provider. Software wallets may be hosted or unhosted. Many unhosted wallet providers will not be considered money transmitters or virtual asset service providers (VASPs) subject to record keeping and reporting requirements like other financial institutions. Unhosted wallets create a situation similar to an individual carrying cash in a billfold or storing it under a mattress. To connect an individual to a billfold full of cash or an unhosted wallet, law enforcement must associate the individual to the assets in some way, such as physical possession or control of the wallet or through transaction tracing back to a point of attribution. The way unhosted wallet software is designed can vary and affect what type of transactional information may be available. In the case of such non-custodial or unhosted wallets, investigators may be dependent on the owner's willingness to cooperate, or the discovery of keys, seeds, and login passwords during device and house searches to access these wallets.

2. Mixing-enabled wallets

The custodial nature of many dedicated mixing services raises significant trust issues for individuals. Is the service going to run off with the money? Will it run into technical difficulties and prevent the funds from being returned? Will the service providers comply with law enforcement or—worse—will law enforcement seize the service?

For the criminal who cannot move past these questions, other mixing options exist in the form of mixing-enabled wallets (MEWs). MEWs may be hosted or unhosted. MEWs integrate a mixing protocol into the wallet so that the end user can automatically, or have the option to, mix their funds before withdrawal. Unhosted MEWs may involve a fee paid to an administrative entity for coordinating the mixing across its user base.

These protocols and proofs, when integrated with a service or software, enable the laundering of funds in an automated fashion and do not offer another financially beneficial function. This makes these services particularly attractive for criminals wishing to conceal or disguise the nature, location, source, ownership, or control of illicit proceeds. The use of mixing services or MEWs could arguably provide evidence of concealment.

B. Institutional exchanges

One of the first exchanges was the infamous Mt. Gox, a fantasy card trading platform that morphed into the world's largest cryptocurrency exchange at the time. Led by French programmer Mark Karpeles, Mt. Gox dominated the early cryptocurrency market, handling an estimated 70% of all transactions on the Bitcoin blockchain. Things didn't go well for Karpeles. The company closed in early 2014 after an estimated 744,000 bitcoins—about 6% of the total 12.4 million bitcoins in circulation at the time—were stolen from the company's wallets. Karpeles was eventually prosecuted by Japanese authorities for falsifying data related to the exchange's accounts.

From this inauspicious beginning, cryptocurrency exchanges became a mainstream platform through which cryptocurrency can be bought, sold, and custodied. Cryptocurrency exchanges operate like online banks. Customers open accounts with a variety of identification documents, and once verified, they can exchange fiat money for cryptocurrency, and vice-versa. While exchanges look and feel like online banks, they typically service a much broader set of customers. Most banks have some connection to their customers' physical location, even if it is an international bank. Customers typically have to open accounts in-person at a bank branch, and a routing number associated with that branch is assigned to the customers' accounts. This is not so with exchanges, which may service customers throughout the world without any physical connection to the location of the exchange. Indeed, exchanges do not have brick and mortar branches where know-your-customer checks can be conducted. Rather, a customer will typically onboard by providing identifying information over the internet. This is not to say that institutional exchanges don't conduct KYC checks after an account is opened, but rather that this is never accomplished via an in-person meeting. Even so, institutional exchanges appear to carry less inherent money laundering risk because the business model isn't premised on charging a money laundering premium. Considering the low fees exchanges charge, it makes sense that individuals interested in legally purchasing or transacting in cryptocurrency would turn to an institutional exchange to deal in these virtual assets. The problem with institutional exchanges is when they fail to maintain adequate anti-money laundering controls. Sometimes, this happens because exchanges directly cater to the criminal element, as was the case with BTC-e, but sometimes, it's simply the result of exchanges being inexperienced or unwilling to spend resources on an adequate compliance program. These failures aren't unique to institutional exchanges, as traditional banks have also been prosecuted for engaging in shoddy anti-money laundering practices for decades.

The larger issue associated with institutional exchanges is when they engage in jurisdictional arbitrage. As noted above, because exchanges don't maintain physical bank branches to operate, it's easy for them to "move around." An exchange can base its operations in an offshore jurisdiction with weak anti-money laundering regulations but still service customers throughout the world. While this doesn't make them immune from U.S. regulations if they service U.S. customers, it can make it more difficult for law enforcement to issue service of process on them and to investigate them. In sum, institutional exchanges don't pose an inherent money laundering risk, but the devil is in the details of how they operate. The broad reach of an institutional exchange means that any failures in its anti-money laundering program can be quickly exploited by criminals throughout the world. For this reason, it is crucial that institutional exchanges maintain robust anti-money laundering programs to compensate for the unusually broad reach of customers they service.

C. Over-the-counter brokers

Over-the-counter (OTC) brokers are a type of MSB that facilitate significant trades between buyers and sellers. While OTC traders maintain accounts at one or several exchanges for liquidity purposes, their customers need not register with the exchange. These are also called nested services in that they tend to operate within one or more larger exchanges. Depending on the OTC broker, a customer may only be required to provide minimal or no KYC information. Criminals may seek out OTC traders because they cannot obtain accounts at exchanges or are unwilling to risk having their funds frozen. In its 2020 Crypto Crime Report, Chainalysis identified the "Rogue 100," a group of OTC brokers it believes to be involved in money laundering activity. Chainalysis stated that just the funds received by these 100 OTC brokers "can account for as much as 1% of all Bitcoin activity in a given month." Chainalysis further noted that, "the money laundering infrastructure driven by OTC brokers enables nearly every other type of crime" covered in the report. Kaiko, a cryptocurrency market data provider, estimated that OTC brokers could facilitate the majority of all cryptocurrency trade volume.

OTC broker case study: North Korean thefts

In August 2020, the United States forfeited cryptocurrency accounts related to three North Korean hacking incidents. According to the complaint, the hacker stole over $250 million worth of alternative cryptocurrencies and tokens, including Proton Tokens, PlayGame tokens, and IHT Real Estate Protocol tokens. The hacker then used multiple virtual asset laundering methods to obfuscate his trail, but ultimately, laundered his illicit proceeds through Chinese OTC actors, who failed to keep KYC records. Despite these attempts to launder the funds, law enforcement traced the funds to the forfeited accounts.

D. P2P exchangers and platforms

A man walks into a Starbucks. He is a peer-to-peer cryptocurrency exchanger. He orders a latte, sits down at a table, and waits for his customer to arrive. The customer walks in and sits down; he has a duffle bag containing $100,000 in cash. The exchanger covertly inspects the cash and then sends $100,000 in bitcoin to a wallet address provided by the customer. They wait for the transaction to be confirmed on the blockchain and then part ways. The customer pays a higher exchange rate as the cost of doing business with an exchanger who will not file a SAR on the transaction. No questions asked; no information reported. This may seem far-fetched, but this type of activity happens daily in cities and towns all over the world, in much larger amounts, and these exchangers often operate on either side of the transaction—both buying and selling millions of dollars' worth of cryptocurrency. It is an effective money laundering scheme unless the P2P exchanger or his customers seeking to stay anonymous get caught.

The business model of P2P exchanging is premised on money laundering. This doesn't mean that all P2P exchangers are money launderers, but rather that the success of the business model depends on it. Otherwise, why would anyone go through the hassle of meeting someone in person to buy or sell cryptocurrency when they could do it online through a registered exchange? On top of the hassle, most exchanges charge less than 2% per transaction, while P2P exchangers often charge between two and six times that rate. Even worse than the hassle and cost, individuals risk being robbed while engaging in face-to-face exchanges. Customers endure this risk, cost, and hassle because they want no questions asked when they buy or sell cryptocurrency—they do not want to provide identification to an exchange, and they do not want a financial institution filing a SAR or a CTR. In other words, they are willing to pay a money laundering premium. Both FinCEN's Advisory and the FATF guidance on money laundering red flags in cryptocurrency transactions include this exact scenario as a red flag, namely, when a P2P exchanger "handle[s] huge amount[s] of [cryptocurrency] transfers on its customer's behalf, and charge[s] higher fees to its customer than transmission services offered by other exchanges." This premium keeps the business model going, as P2P exchangers continue to operate illegally even with the risk of civil or criminal fines under the money laundering statutes and the Bank Secrecy Act.

In addition to criminals, victims of ransomware attacks have relied on P2P exchangers. With the rise of ransomware as a standardized criminal enterprise, an increasing number of victims have been forced to purchase cryptocurrency in short order. It has been estimated that 9% of Bitcoin transactions are attributable to ransomware or some other form of cyber extortion payment. If it takes days or weeks to open a validated account at an institutional exchange, a P2P exchanger can offer cryptocurrency at a moment's notice, and victims are willing to pay this speed premium. Victims have noted that "the processing times [at a registered institutional exchange] were far beyond the scope of the immediacy posed by the ransom" and that a P2P exchanger was a better option for obtaining cryptocurrency in a hurry.

Law enforcement has successfully prosecuted P2P exchangers for money laundering and violations of the BSA, but these cases are exceptions to the norm of P2P exchangers operating with impunity. Law enforcement has limited resources and simply cannot investigate every P2P exchanger operating outside of the law. Another method for dealing with P2P money laundering is focusing on the platforms used by P2P exchangers. These platforms often operate like Craigslist, allowing P2P exchangers to advertise cryptocurrency they want to buy or sell. Most of these services operate an escrow service for transactions conducted through the site to minimize scamming. Without these sites, P2P exchangers would struggle to advertise their services and conduct trades in an efficient manner. In return for providing these services, P2P exchange sites often charge a fixed or percentage-based fee for every transaction conducted through their platforms.

By not just passively providing a communication forum, these sites may be considered money transmitters subject to the Bank Secrecy Act and related regulations. Moreover, sites offering custodial, or hosted, wallets are more likely money services businesses (MSBs) under the law in the United States and VASPs according to the FATF Recommendations. Customers of these platforms pay a premium for anonymity, and KYC policies defeat the anonymity that many customers seek, which is why these platforms rarely maintain robust compliance programs. Stronger enforcement measures against these (i) exchange between virtual assets and fiat currencies, (ii) exchange between one or more forms of virtual assets, (iii) transfer of virtual assets, (iv) safekeeping and/or administration of virtual assets or instruments enabling control over virtual assets, and (v) participation in and provision of financial services related to an issuer's offer and/or sale of a virtual asset.").

In 2018, the Department of Justice (Department) and multiple federal law enforcement agencies announced the results of a year-long, coordinated national operation dubbed Operation Dark Gold. Investigators used the popular P2P exchanger business model to target vendors of illicit goods on the Darknet. Posing as a cryptocurrency money launderer on Darknet market websites, undercover investigators exchanged U.S. currency for cryptocurrency with numerous vendors of illicit goods, leading to the identification and prosecution of scores of these individuals across the country. The undercover exchanger received cash from these criminals through the mail, and investigators were able trace the cryptocurrency received from them back to their illicit activities. In addition to the take down of these targeted vendors, the Department seized over $25 million in cash, gold, and cryptocurrency, as well as drugs, guns, and a grenade launcher.

E. Mixing services

In the 1990s, groups of tax dodgers began using a scheme called warehouse banking, in which a dirty bank would commingle all deposits into a single account to conceal the ownership of the funds. When a depositor withdrew funds from the account, it was impossible to trace where those funds came from. Eventually, these schemes were shut down, and the organizers were prosecuted for tax and money laundering violations. Mixing services are the warehouse banking of cryptocurrency: Funds are sent to the mixing service, where they are commingled with other funds and then sent to a designated wallet address in the same or different form of cryptocurrency. While these services claim to have legitimate purposes, such as enhancing a user's privacy while engaging in cryptocurrency transactions, money laundering is a main component of their operations.

Even with a business model based on money laundering, mixing services may be obligated to maintain anti-money laundering programs and respond to records requests from law enforcement. As such, they aren't always a black box for law enforcement and may in fact provide useful information for criminal investigations. All of the risks associated with institutional exchanges also exist with mixing services: They can jurisdiction hop; they can service clients globally; and they likely lack the necessary anti-money laundering (AML) compliance systems and staff to keep up with inherent risks in their business model. Nevertheless, it is theoretically possible that a mixing service could comply with U.S. regulations if it maintained a sufficient anti-money laundering program.

Mixing services case study: Bitcoin Fog

In April 2021, federal prosecutors charged a dual Russian–Swedish national for his alleged operation of the longest-running bitcoin money laundering service on the Darknet. According to court documents, the defendant operated

163

Bitcoin Fog, a cryptocurrency "mixer," gaining notoriety as a go-to money laundering service for criminals seeking to hide their illicit proceeds from law enforcement. The criminal complaint filed in the District of Columbia alleged that since 2011, Bitcoin Fog moved over 1.2 million bitcoin—valued at approximately $335 million at the time of the transactions, and the bulk of this cryptocurrency came from Darknet marketplaces and was tied to illegal products and services.

F. Cryptocurrency kiosks

It is estimated that, as of April 2021, there are over 19,000 cryptocurrency kiosks globally. Like other high-risk cryptocurrency platforms, cryptocurrency kiosks may provide an effective vehicle for money laundering. Kiosks operate like ATM machines. Customers go to physical machines, often located in easily accessible locations like shopping malls or gas stations, and use the machines to purchase or sell cryptocurrency. Customers often pay exorbitant premiums to use kiosks, much like the premiums charged by P2P exchangers. Because cryptocurrency kiosks have only recently become popular, enforcement actions have been rare. Until the cryptocurrency kiosk industry has been educated, and perhaps tamed, by regulators and law enforcement, it will remain a popular tool for a wide variety of criminal activity. Kiosks have been heavily used by individuals and entities that promote, facilitate, and profit from sex trafficking because cryptocurrency has increasingly been used to pay for websites that advertise commercial sex. One of the reasons for the increased use of cryptocurrency is that major merchant processors, like Visa and Mastercard, no longer allow transactions to pay for or host advertisements websites, such as the government-seized Backpage. In some cases, traffickers or victims of trafficking under the direction of their trafficker will change the form of the illicit proceeds from cash to cryptocurrency at kiosks and then use the cryptocurrency to further promote the illegal activity.

Another reason why traffickers prefer using cryptocurrency kiosks is their ability to avoid the KYC requirements of regulated institutional exchanges. While kiosk companies fall squarely within the same set of BSA regulations, they often operate without sufficient AML controls. This allows their customers to carry out transactions, particularly small ones that are used to pay for advertisements for commercial sex, without providing any identification. Often, victims of sex trafficking may not have access to bank accounts, or in some instances, traffickers open bank accounts using the victims' names. By using kiosks, the traffickers can also avoid linking any bank accounts or a financial footprint as would be required if they used traditional financial institutions or institutional exchanges.

Kiosks are also commonly used by dark web market vendors of illicit products, including drugs, firearms, and stolen identity information, who are looking to offload the payments they received from customers in cryptocurrency. They can tolerate the high premiums as a reasonable price to pay for anonymity. Moreover, operating one or more kiosks may offer such vendors a lucrative method for converting illicit proceeds from cryptocurrency back into fiat currency. This isn't to say that vendors only use kiosks. Rather, vendors often use the full scope of domains described in this article. If one of their accounts is closed, they can easily move to another domain.

Finally, kiosks may facilitate cryptocurrency payments in fraud and extortion schemes in which victims are directed to use kiosks to easily and quickly obtain and send cryptocurrency to perpetrators. In sum, cryptocurrency kiosks are high-risk enterprises, even with robust compliance programs.

G. Traditional financial institutions

Traditional financial institutions often play a significant role in cryptocurrency money laundering because, in the end, criminals want to convert their ill-gotten cryptocurrency into fiat currency—and the most useful and common place to maintain fiat currency is in a depository institution. When ill-gotten funds are converted to fiat currency and sent to a bank for safekeeping, criminals can continue to layer (by sending the funds to other locations) or they can begin the integration process (by purchasing goods or paying off debts).

Banks will often see funds sent to or from institutional exchanges because the exchanges often require customers to provide a bank account as part of the onboarding process. The exchange customer uses the linked bank account to pay for cryptocurrency purchases and to receive the proceeds of cryptocurrency sales. This activity should be easy for a bank to identify, as it can determine if the recipient is an institutional exchange. Based on this information, the bank can make individualized risk assessments about its customers. As such, a bank with a sufficient compliance program should be able to incur tolerable risk when servicing customers engaged in cryptocurrency transactions.

A bank's risk levels may increase, however, if its customers are P2P exchangers, who often use banks to send or receive payments (or to deposit or withdraw cash). A robust AML program should pick up on a customer engaged in this type of activity because it will trigger red flags, including unexplained cash deposits and withdrawals and wire transfers with unknown business purposes. This type of suspicious conduct should cause a bank to inquire with the customer as to the source of funds. If the customer can't explain her business practices, the accounts likely should be closed by the bank.

What are the common financial patterns of P2P exchangers? It depends on if they are selling or buying cryptocurrency, though, often, they will do both as a means of triaging bear and bull cryptocurrency markets. If the P2P exchanger is purchasing cryptocurrency from customers, bank records will show a wire transfer or other payment method to a series of random individuals (the P2P exchanger's customers). Without additional information about the customer, it might be difficult for the bank to determine the purpose of such debits. In addition to direct payments, P2P exchangers will also operate in cash. This means that their bank accounts will often show regular, large cash deposits or withdrawals. After the P2P exchanger purchases the cryptocurrency, she may send it to an institutional exchange, where it will be sold. The profits are then transferred back to the P2P exchanger's bank account. It is not uncommon, therefore, for P2P exchangers to regularly receive large domestic and international wire transfers from institutional exchanges.

If the P2P exchanger is selling cryptocurrency, she will likely receive regular payments from customers or make regular cash deposits into her accounts. Sometimes that deposited cash is used to buy more cryptocurrency from an institutional exchange, and the cycle begins again. But as noted above, P2P exchangers will often both buy and sell cryptocurrency, so their bank account records will likely show a combination of these transaction patterns.

Should a bank automatically close an account when it learns that a customer is a P2P exchanger? No single answer is correct. It is, in theory, possible for a P2P exchanger to operate within the law. She would have to be a licensed money transmitter, both federally and at the state level; would have to maintain an anti-money laundering compliance program; and would have to file SARs and CTRs. If all these requirements are met, a bank might be able to justify the potential risks of servicing a customer engaged in this business activity.

H. Cryptocurrency debit cards and payment apps

Just as criminals have used credit cards, debit cards, and gift cards to facilitate unlawful activity, conceal illicit financial flows, and use these methods of payment to integrate ill-gotten gains, debit cards and payment apps funded by or supporting cryptocurrency transactions may also be used to launder money.

Cryptocurrency payment processors operate in a familiar manner to other fiat-sourced payment apps. These companies provide software allowing retail merchants to accept cryptocurrencies as payment online or in brick-and-mortar establishments. Generally, the merchants do not handle cryptocurrencies directly. Rather, customers fund their payment app wallet or debit card with cryptocurrency, and the processor converts the cryptocurrency into fiat currency. The processor then sends those converted funds to the merchant, minus a commission. Like exchanges and kiosks, most payment processors are MSBs with BSA record keeping and reporting requirements.

Thus, their KYC and transactional records can be an important source for leads and evidence in financial investigations.

Examples of established fiat payment processors now offering varying services in cryptocurrency are PayPal (including Venmo) and Square (d/b/a CashApp). Many national retailers like Home Depot and Whole Foods accept Flexa, a payments network supported by various cryptocurrency payment apps. In addition, many companies, including exchanges and payment processors, offer visa debit cards funded with cryptocurrency account balances. Like fiat-funded debit cards, these cards can be used to pay for anything online or in person or used to make ATM cash withdrawals. For a more detailed discussion of these new technologies, the authors recommend Money Moves: Following the Money Beyond the Banking System.

I. Cryptocurrency gambling websites

These online gambling platforms or "casinos" that facilitate various forms of betting denominated in bitcoin and other cryptocurrencies are increasingly used for money laundering. Under current law, a casino that has gross annual gaming revenue in excess of $1 million, regardless of denomination in cryptocurrency or other value, must be duly licensed and authorized to do business as a casino in the

United States by a federal, State, or tribal authority. Casinos that do not meet this criterion may be considered MSBs and subject to the BSA and its KYC record keeping and reporting requirements, nonetheless.

Criminals may launder their illicit proceeds through cryptocurrency gambling sites as a layering technique. On these sites, users may send their dirty cryptocurrency to the online casino, trading them for virtual chips or credit. Whether the criminal chooses to gamble any of their funds is up to them, but otherwise the virtual chips or credit may then be cashed out into a virtual asset and withdrawn.

V. Following the crypto: potential on-chain layering techniques

A. A note on blockchain analysis

It is possible, using the Bitcoin blockchain, to trace funds forwards and backwards from a single address or a single transaction, not unlike the manner in which investigators trace the movement of funds in fiat currencies. Unlike a traditional bank statement, however, the record on a blockchain for a particular bitcoin address often contains only a single incoming and single outgoing transaction, due to the practice of depositing leftover funds in a new change address. In these instances, it becomes necessary to identify the sequence of subsequent and prior payments to trace the disposition of funds associated with a single actor. Additionally, unlike more traditional bank records, the blockchain does not identify the sender or receiver, apart from the public addresses. Investigators can sometimes obtain this information from serving legal process to MSBs and VASPs. In this way, it is often possible for investigators to identify payment streams—that is, a single flow of funds over time—believed to involve the same pool of funds controlled by a particular person or persons. As a result, blockchain analysis is a crucial technique for investigating virtual assets.

One of the most common techniques involved in blockchain analysis is co-spend analysis, sometimes referred to as "common input analysis." Co-spending occurs when multiple inputs are used to send bitcoin in a single transaction, indicating that a single owner holds the private keys for all those addresses.

For example, six disparate Bitcoin addresses found in an investigation may, on their face, appear unrelated. A quick search of an open source blockchain explorer reveals transactions associated with these addresses. But what can those transactions tell us? By analyzing the transactions using co-spend analysis, the investigator may connect the dots to determine that all the addresses belong to the same wallet.

But what if the investigator were to find an additional transaction involving three inputs from an address in each of the above wallets?

The investigator may then demonstrate that each of the original six disparate addresses are a part of the same wallet. This analytic technique, when combined with traditional investigative steps, may provide valuable insight. Armed with blockchain analysis and traditional investigative tools, investigators may leverage this information to determine the breadth of the scheme, the value of the assets, cash out points, and even the identity of criminal actors.

B. Anonymity and privacy-enhanced cryptocurrencies

Sometimes, the money laundering vehicle is the cryptocurrency itself. As detailed above, while Bitcoin provides for a public and transparent blockchain, a number of cryptocurrencies are designed with blockchains that enhance the privacy of transactions; these cryptocurrencies are often referred to as anonymity-enhanced cryptocurrencies (AECs) or privacy coins. The Department considers the use of AECs to be indicative of possible criminal conduct and generally does not liquidate seized or forfeited AECs.

Although cryptocurrency addresses do not have names or specific customer information attached to them, because many blockchains are public, users can query addresses to view and understand the transactions to some extent. AECs, however, use non-public or private blockchains, or built-in mixing protocols, that make it more difficult to trace or attribute transactions. Like sharks to chum, criminals seek out privacy to conceal their conduct, and AECs offer these additional features for concealing value transfer. In terms of the PLI process, AECs make layering inherent to all transactions and, therefore, are an efficient method for this part of the money laundering process.

AECs and privacy coins may use various non-interactive zero-knowledge proofs as a part of the underlying technology to facilitate the transfer of value. For example, ZCash private and shielded transactions use zero-knowledge succinct non-interactive argument of knowledge (zk-SNARK) proofs to encrypt the involved private address(es). Private transactions will also encrypt the transaction amount and memo field. Monero uses Bulletproofs, another type of non-interactive zero-knowledge proof. Non-interactive zero knowledge proofs are a type of zero-knowledge proof in which the prover sends one message to the verifier in which the prover demonstrates to the verifier that they know something. This is done without the prover conveying any information apart from the fact that they know that something. When applied to the cryptocurrency space, this means that specific information about a transaction need not be given away, apart from a representation of ownership of funds.

C. Mixing

In a nutshell, successful mixing breaks any links between the originator and the destination. There are several different protocols that may change the way the mixing is accomplished. One of the more commonly exploited by criminal actors is CoinJoin.

CoinJoin is a trustless method for combining multiple payments from multiple spenders into a single transaction with multiple outputs, making it more difficult for outside parties to determine which spender paid which recipient or recipients.

D. Chain hopping

The concept of layering is not new to criminals. This can take many forms in the traditional financial world, including wire transfers between bank accounts, often held in multiple names, at multiple banks, and in multiple countries or real estate investments. Within the virtual asset landscape, one of the more prominent forms of layering is known as chain hopping or swapping. This involves switching from one cryptocurrency or virtual asset, such as a token, to another to break the chain. By trading one type of virtual asset for another, the criminal switches blockchains, attempting to obfuscate the transaction origin and destination. This is generally done via dedicated centralized services or in an automated fashion (for example, decentralized exchanges).

Bibliography

Ablan, J., Stempel, J., "Buffett bashes bitcoin as thriving on mystique, favors stocks, Reuters", May 7, 2018, https://www.reuters.com/article/us-berkshire-buffett-cnbc/buffett-bashes-bitcoin-as-thriving-on-mystique-favors-stocks-idINKBN1I813F

Backman, M., "Is Bitcoin Safer for Retirement Than Social Security?", May 21, 2021, https://www.fool.com/retirement/2021/05/21/is-bitcoin-safer-for-retirement-than-social-securi/

Ballotpedia , "Nevada Gaming Tax Increase on Monthly Revenue above $250,000 Initiative (2022)", Ballotpedia, 2021, https://ballotpedia.org/Nevada_Gaming_Tax_Increase_on_Monthly_Revenue_above_$250,000_Initiative_(2022)

Bank for International Settlements, "Annual Economic Report 2018", https://www.bis.org/publ/arpdf/ar2018e.htm

Batabyal, A. , "How To Create Your Own Cryptocurrency In 15 Minutes - Learn Step-by-Step", Apr. 30 2020, https://coinswitch.co/news/how-to-create-your-own-cryptocurrency-in-15-minutes-learn-step-by-step

Bennington, A., "Bitcoin Bear Peter Schiff Doubles Down: Even at $4,000 It's Still a 'Bubble'", Ash Bennington, Aug. 17, 2017, https://www.coindesk.com/bitcoin-bear-peter-schiff-doubles-even-4000-still-bubble

Bhutoria, R., "Bitcoin Investment Thesis, Bitcoin's Role As An Alternative Investment", Fidelity Digital Assets, Oct. 2020, https://www.fidelitydigitalassets.com/bin-public/060_www_fidelity_com/documents/FDAS/bitcoin-alternative-investment.pdf

Bloomenthal, A., "What Determines the Price of 1 Bitcoin?", Investopedia, May 19, 2021, https://www.investopedia.com/tech/what-determines-value-1-bitcoin/

Buttonwood, "Greater fool theory. The bitcoin bubble", The Economist, Nov. 1, 2017, https://www.economist.com/buttonwoods-notebook/2017/11/01/the-bitcoin-bubble

Cambridge, "Bitcoin Electricity Consumption Index", May 2021, https://cbeci.org/cbeci/comparisons

Chancellor, E., "Bitcoin speculators face total wipeout", Reuters, Dec. 13, 2017, https://cn.reuters.com/article/us-markets-bitcoin-breakingviews-idUSKBN1E721S

Conlon, T, McGee, R. "Safe haven or risky hazard? Bitcoin during the Covid-19 bear market", Finance Research Letters, May 21, 2020, https://doi.org/10.1016/j.frl.2020.101607

Davies, G., "A History of Money", Revised and updated by Duncan Connors, 4th edition. Cardiff: University of Wales Press, 2016

Department of Justice, "Report of The Attorney General's Cyberdigital Task Force", U.S. Department of Justice Office of the Deputy Attorney General Cyber-Digital Task Force, Oct., 2020, https://www.justice.gov/archives/ag/page/file/1326061/download

Economist, "Crypto-miners are probably to blame for the graphics-chip shortage", The Economist, June 19, 2021, https://www.economist.com/graphic-detail/2021/06/19/crypto-miners-are-probably-to-blame-for-the-graphics-chip-shortage

Eichengreen, B., "International Currencies in the Lens of History", in S. Battilossi, Y. Cassis and K. Yago (eds.), Handbook of the History of Money and Currency. Singapore: Springer, 2020, pp. 335–59.

Elliott R., Vigna, P., "Elon Musk Says Tesla Suspends Accepting Bitcoin for Vehicle Purchases", Wall Street Journal, May 12, 2021, https://www.wsj.com/articles/elon-musk-says-tesla-suspends-accepting-bitcoin-for-vehicle-purchases-11620858838

Gemini, The State of U.S. Crypto Report, Apr. 2021, https://www.gemini.com/state-of-us-crypto

Green, M., "The Case Against Bitcoin", May 14, 2021, https://bariweiss.substack.com/p/the-case-against-bitcoin

Grym, A. "The great illusion of digital currencies", BoF Economics Review, No. 1/2018, Bank of Finland, June 21, 2018, http://nbn-resolving.de/urn:NBN:fi:bof-201806211659

Hajric, V. "Canadian issuer is making its Bitcoin ETF carbon-neutral", Financial Post, May 10, 2021, https://financialpost.com/fp-finance/cryptocurrency/canadian-issuer-is-making-its-bitcoin-etf-carbon-neutral

Jevons, W.S., "Money and the Mechanism of Exchange", New York: D. Appleton & Co. (1875)

Kharpal, A., Bitcoin price will crash to zero, Nouriel Roubini says, CNBC, Feb. 6, 2018, https://www.cnbc.com/2018/02/06/bitcoin-price-will-crash-to-zero-nouriel-roubini-says.html

Kharif, O., "Bitcoin Whales' Ownership Concentration Is Rising During Rally", Bloomberg, Nov. 18, 2020, https://www.bloomberg.com/news/articles/2020-11-18/bitcoin-whales-ownership-concentration-is-rising-during-rally

Klein, T., Thu, H.P., Walther, T., 2018, "Bitcoin is not the New Gold – A comparison of volatility, correlation, and portfolio performance", International Review of Financial Analysis, Vol. 59, pp. 105-116.

La Roche, J., "Bitcoin: There is a massive manipulation by a bunch of whales... it's a risky asset class: Roubini", Yahoo Finance, Feb. 22, 2021, https://m.youtube.com/watch?v=IlIImMvvOEo

La Roche, J., " 'Retail suckers' with FOMO will eventually get crushed on Bitcoin, says Roubini", Yahoo Finance, Feb. 22, 2021, https://ca.yahoo.com/finance/news/nouriel-roubini-on-bitcoin-price-surge-215856375.html

Lahart, J., "If Crypto Crashes Tomorrow, It's No Big Deal. In Five Years, It Might Be", Wall Street Journal, May 7, 2021, https://www.wsj.com/articles/cryptocurrency-crash-no-big-deal-bitcoin-ether-dogecoin-11620332378

Lee, J. "Research Affiliates Quant Warns of Bitcoin Market Manipulation", Bloomberg, Jan. 14, 2021, https://www.bloomberg.com/news/articles/2021-01-14/research-affiliates-quant-warns-of-bitcoin-market-manipulation

Mackintosh, J., "Bitcoin's Reliance on Stablecoins Harks Back to the Wild West of Finance", Wall Street Journal, May 27, 2021, https://www.wsj.com/articles/bitcoins-reliance-on-stablecoins-harks-back-to-the-wild-west-of-finance-11622115246

Makori, M., "Bitcoin will never be 'digital gold' and Central Bank Digital Currencies will kill cryptos – Roubini", Kitco News, May 10, 2021, https://www.youtube.com/watch?v=yL0QcyQwdBo

Nakamoto, S., "Bitcoin: A Peer-to-Peer Electronic Cash System", Jan. 2009, https://bitcoin.org/bitcoin.pdf

Nasdaq, "Manipulation in Cryptocurrency Markets: Top 3 Behaviors to Monitor", Nasdaq, May 2021, https://www.nasdaq.com/solutions/nasdaq-market-surveillance

Parfomak, P., "Colonial Pipeline - The DarkSide Strikes, Congressional Research Service", May 11, 2021, https://crsreports.congress.gov/product/pdf/IN/IN11667

Popper, N. "Bitcoin Has Lost Steam. But Criminals Still Love It", The New York Times, Jan. 28, 2020, https://www.nytimes.com/2020/01/28/technology/bitcoin-black-market.html

Pound, J., "SEC Chairman Gary Gensler says more investor protections are needed for bitcoin and crypto markets", CNBC, May 7, 2021, https://www.cnbc.com/2021/05/07/sec-chairman-gary-gensler-says-more-investor-protections-are-needed-for-bitcoin-and-crypto-markets.html

Prasad, E., "The Brutal Truth about BitCoin", The New York Times, June 15, 2021, https://www.nytimes.com/2021/06/14/opinion/bitcoin-cryptocurrency-flaws.html

Reuters, "China bans financial institutions from offering cryptocurrency services", Financial Post, May 18, 2021, https://financialpost.com/fp-finance/cryptocurrency/china-bans-financial-payment-institutions-from-cryptocurrency-business

Roubini, N., "Interview with Nouriel Roubini", in Crypto: A New Class of Asset?, Global Macro Research, Issue 98, Goldman Sachs, (2021), https://www.goldmansachs.com/insights/pages/crypto-a-new-asset-class-f/report.pdf

Roubini, N., "Crypto is the Mother of All Scams and (Now Busted) Bubbles - While Blockchain Is The Most Over-Hyped Technology Ever, No Better than a Spreadsheet/Database (Book Edition)", May 2021, https://bitsblocks.github.io/crypto-bubbles

Rooney, K, "Bitcoin is the 'mother of all scams' and blockchain is most hyped tech ever, Roubini tells Congress" , Oct. 12, 2018, https://www.cnbc.com/2018/10/11/roubini-bitcoin-is-mother-of-all-scams.html

Sarin, A, "Bitcoin is close to becoming worthless", MarketWatch, Dec. 4, 2018, https://www.marketwatch.com/story/bitcoin-is-close-to-becoming-worthless-2018-12-03

Shifflett, S., Vigna P, "Traders Are Talking Up Cryptocurrencies, Then Dumping Them, Costing Others Millions", Wall Street Journal, Aug. 5. 2018, https://www.wsj.com/graphics/cryptocurrency-schemes-generate-big-coin/

Shin, H. S., "Cryptocurrencies: looking beyond the hype, BIS Annual Economic Report", June 17, 2018, https://www.bis.org/publ/arpdf/ar2018e5.htm

Smith, J., "Treasury calls for doubling IRS staff to target tax evasion, crypto transfers", Yahoo Finance, May 20, 2021, https://finance.yahoo.com/news/treasury-calls-for-doubling-irs-staff-to-target-tax-evasion-crypto-transfers-164840153.html

SoFi, "How to Get a Bitcoin (BTC) Loan", (2020) https://www.sofi.com/learn/content/how-to-get-bitcoin-loan/

Stankiewicz, K, "'Black Swan' author calls bitcoin a 'gimmick' and a 'game,' says it resembles a Ponzi scheme", CNBC, Apr. 23, 2021, https://www.cnbc.com/2021/04/23/bitcoin-a-gimmick-and-resembles-a-ponzi-scheme-black-swan-author-.html

Svensson, R., "Economic Perspectives of Numismatics", Stockholm: The Swedish Numismatic Society, 2021

Svensson, R., "Bitcoin lacks a solid foundation as an international currency", Financial Times, June 7 2021, https://www.ft.com/content/aee87c1d-b00f-4c22-ab97-97bb2b042342

Vildana H., "Canadian issuer is making its Bitcoin ETF carbon-neutral", May 10, 2021 https://financialpost.com/fp-finance/cryptocurrency/canadian-issuer-is-making-its-bitcoin-etf-carbon-neutral

Watson, P., "Why Bitcoin Can't Be Money, Connecting the Dots", Maudlin Economics, Dec. 12, 2017, https://www.mauldineconomics.com/connecting-the-dots/why-bitcoin-cant-be-money

Wayt, T., "Regulators in 'sprint' to crack down on cryptocurrencies, Fed official says", NY Post, May 26, 2021, https://nypost.com/2021/05/26/regulators-in-sprint-to-crackdown-on-cryptocurrencies-fed-official-says/

Weatherford, J., "The History of Money", New York: Three Rivers Press, 1997.

Weisenthal, J., "How Bitcoin Is Like North Korea", Jan. 12, 2014, https://www.businessinsider.com/bitcoin-inequality-2014-1

Wikipedia, "List of countries by wealth inequality", May 2021, https://en.wikipedia.org/wiki/List_of_countries_by_wealth_inequality

6park news, "Bitcoin plunged again 'Doctor Doom' warns: Bitcoin price is subject to large-scale manipulation", Feb. 22, 2021, https://6park.news/en/bitcoin-plunged-again-doctor-doom-warns-bitcoin-price-is-subject-to-large-scale-manipulation-digital-currency-blockchain.html

Appendices

A – "Attorney General William P. Barr Announces Publication of Cryptocurrency Enforcement Framework", Department of Justice, Oct. 8 2020, https://www.justice.gov/opa/pr/attorney-general-william-p-barr-announces-publication-cryptocurrency-enforcement-framework

B – "Owner of Bitcoin Exchange Sentenced to Prison for Money Laundering, Department of Justice", Jan. 12 2021, https://www.justice.gov/opa/pr/owner-bitcoin-exchange-sentenced-prison-money-laundering

C – "Customer Advisory: Understand the Risks of Virtual Currency Trading", Commodity Futures Trading Commission, May 23 2021, https://www.cftc.gov/LearnAndProtect/AdvisoriesAndArticles/understand_risks_of_virtual_currency.html

D – "Court Authorizes Service of John Doe Summons Seeking Identities of U.S. Taxpayers Who Have Used Cryptocurrency", Department of Justice, May 5, 2021, https://www.justice.gov/opa/pr/court-authorizes-service-john-doe-summons-seeking-identities-us-taxpayers-who-have-used-1

E – "Federal Court Orders UK Man to Pay More Than $571 Million for Operating Fraudulent Bitcoin Trading Scheme, Commodity Futures Trading Commission", Mar. 26 2021, https://www.cftc.gov/PressRoom/PressReleases/8371-21

F – "The Financial Crimes Enforcement Network Proposes Rule Aimed at Closing Anti-Money Laundering Regulatory Gaps for Certain Convertible Virtual Currency and Digital Asset Transactions", Department of the Treasury, Dec. 18 2020, https://home.treasury.gov/news/press-releases/sm1216

G – "Thinking About Buying the Latest New Cryptocurrency or Token?", U.S. Securities and Exchange Commission, May 2021, https://www.investor.gov/additional-resources/spotlight/directors-take/thinking-about-buying-latest-new-cryptocurrency-or

H – "FOR SALE Approximately 4,041.58424932 bitcoin", United States Marshal, Feb. 2020, https://www.usmarshals.gov/assets/2020/febbitcoinauction/

I – "Surfing the First Wave of Cryptocurrency Money Laundering", DOJ Journal of Federal Law and Practice, May 2021, https://www.justice.gov/file/1403666/download

Acknowledgments

We would like to acknowledge and thank all those who assisted us to write this book including: Nicola Mahaffy and Elisabeth Gustafsson who took our photographs; and, Angelo Giordano who took the front cover photograph.

Printed in Great Britain
by Amazon

64922443R00102